SHAKER MINIATURE FURNITURE

SHAKER MINIATURE FURNITURE

Cynthia and Jerome Rubin

VNR **VAN NOSTRAND REINHOLD COMPANY**
New York Cincinnati Toronto London Melbourne

Photographs by Michael Rizza

Copyright © 1979 by Cynthia Rubin and Jerome Rubin
Library of Congress Catalog Card Number 78-15500
ISBN 0-442-27150-6

Published in 1979 by Van Nostrand Reinhold Company
A division of Litton Educational Publishing, Inc.
135 West 50th Street, New York, NY 10020, U.S.A.

Van Nostrand Reinhold Limited
1410 Birchmount Road
Scarborough, Ontario M1P 2E7, Canada

Van Nostrand Reinhold Australia Pty. Ltd.
17 Queen Street
Mitcham, Victoria 3132, Australia

Van Nostrand Reinhold Company Limited
Molly Millars Lane
Wokingham, Berkshire, England

16 15 14 13 12 11 10 9 8 7 6 5 4 3 2 1

Library of Congress Cataloging in Publication Data

Rubin, Cynthia.
  Shaker miniature furniture.

  Bibliography: p.
  Includes index.
  1. Miniature craft. 2. Miniature furniture.
3. Furniture, Shaker. I. Rubin, Jerome, joint
author. II. Title.
TT178.R8   684.1′04′0974   78-15500
ISBN 0-442-27150-6

To Alice and Gus
who encouraged us in our love for
Shaker miniature furniture

Contents

Preface

Reflecting America's heritage in miniature is a rewarding hobby, and now, for the first time, the world of the Shaker miniature is available for dedicated miniature enthusiasts. With this book, containing measured drawings (in the scale of one inch equals one foot) based on our collection of Shaker miniature furniture, we have tried to give miniature enthusiasts a background and understanding of not only Shaker design but also the Shaker lifestyle. We do not pretend to give a thoroughly detailed history of Shaker culture nor a substitution for the personal experience provided by visiting a Shaker museum or restoration, but we can offer you an appreciation and basis from which you can start your own adventure with Shaker miniature furniture.

Unlike other periods of American decorative arts, to fully understand the simplicity and form of Shaker furniture, you must understand the Shaker philosophy. In no other field of Americana is the relationship between religion and artifacts so close and intermingled. Shakerism is not an endproduct of any singular idea; it is a unique and self-sustaining American utopian quest whose furniture and interior design reflect the individuality of the evolving movement.

Although this religious society believed in separation from non-Shakers or the "outside world," so influential was its economic policy and so important its many agricultural and manufacturing activities that Shakerism influenced opinion and practice throughout America's formation until the early twentieth century. Our debt to the Shakers is just now being recognized. They are credited with inventing a number of important innovations, including the threshing machine, an improved commercial washing machine, the circular saw, a pea sheller, an automatic apple parer, the metal pen point or nib, and the flat broom. Also, they are the acknowledged founders of many basic American industries, including the mail-order seed business, the canning industry, and the pharmaceutical industry.

With the incredible growth in interest in the miniature hobby field in recent years, it is only natural that miniature enthusiasts are looking to American forms in furniture—including Shaker design—for ideas and inspiration. As in any field of endeavor that is experiencing rapid growth, there has been a certain amount of experimentation. Our purpose here, however, is to provide a sound basis of understanding on which you can expand, depending on the extent of your expertise and interest. Presented are an awareness of the high caliber of Shaker craftsmanship and authentic miniature reproductions of Shaker design.

Shaker design is characterized by great care of workmanship and attention to detail. A high standard of craftsmanship increased the value and success of Shaker products. Appreciation of the integrity and beauty of Shaker simplicity has grown among miniature enthusiasts.

With the great acceptance of and interest in miniatures throughout the craft world, many talented individuals have discovered the challenge of producing authentic miniature reproductions. Many collections have been richly built by expert craftsmen who have further perpetuated the world of fine workmanship. (Our own collection has been fashioned by a talented craftsman, who, because of the great interest in his work and his own limited output, wishes to remain anonymous.) It must be pointed out that a great deal of satisfaction is derived from creating exceptional pieces that will be enjoyed for generations.

It can also be great fun to visit the many Shaker collections and museums around the country. In their gift shops, Shaker miniatures, the work of contemporary craftspeople, can be purchased; thus fine collections can be started. Our own lives have been greatly enriched by our Shaker miniature interest, and we hope that this book will spark a fruitful interest on your part.

Introduction

Shaker furniture, with its simple and utilitarian lines, lends itself to the craft of miniature furniture making. Since all ornamentation has been eliminated, the furniture's main distinguishing characteristic is functionalism. All pieces of furniture have an important and valid use in their environment. Fine workmanship and sturdy construction are additional distinctive features. A forthright and balanced sense of design add even further dimensions to its outstanding graceful beauty.

Seen against a stark whitewashed background, Shaker furniture gives a peaceful appearance, enhancing its own tranquil surroundings. Fine domestic woods, such as cherry, maple, walnut, and butternut shed a warmth and integrity that helps to give Shaker furniture its current reputation as an important contribution to American decorative arts.

Behind this enduring beauty lies a religious philosophy that provided the motivation for this fine workmanship. In order to fully appreciate Shaker furniture, therefore, you must first understand the story of Shakerism.

It all began in the year 1774 when the impoverished Ann Lee arrived in New York

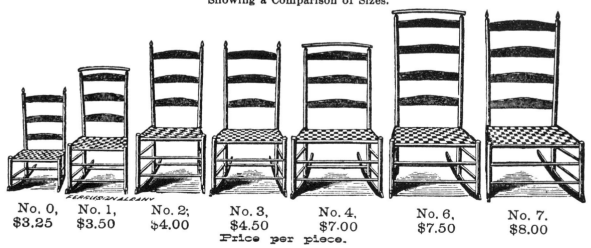

The Shakers' Slat Back Chairs, with Rockers.
WORSTED LACE WEB SEATS.
Showing a Comparison of Sizes.

| No. 0, $3.25 | No. 1, $3.50 | No. 2; $4.00 | No. 3, $4.50 | No. 4, $7.00 | No. 6, $7.50 | No. 7. $8.00 |

Price per piece.

This facsimile of a page from a Shaker chair catalog, circa 1875, indicates the range of sizes and prices for slat-back chairs with rockers. The Shakers at Mt. Lebanon, New York made chairs of this type for the commercial trade from the mid-nineteenth century until the 1920s.

11

from Liverpool with eight loyal followers. Ann Lee was born in Manchester, England in 1737 amidst the poverty and inhumane conditions of the emerging Industrial Revolution. She was a Quaker whose visions and divine revelations were the source of constant persecution and periodic imprisonment in England.

A vision revealed to her that she was the successor to Jesus, the woman incarnate of the word of God, which was again to be given to man during the second coming of Christ. Having attained a spiritual serenity with this knowledge, she turned her attention toward helping others along the same path that had been revealed to her. Another vision instructed her to go to America where she could escape religious persecution and gather her loyal band to live and worship together as they pleased.

These obscure English immigrants arrived in America at a difficult time in its early history since the American patriots were turning against British citizens. Since they had no friends in New York City where they landed, they decided to separate in order to find employment and earn a living. They were eventually reunited on a donated piece of land north of Albany, New York called Niskayuna, an Indian name meaning "good maize land." Five years later, their crude wooden house became an active center during a series of fanatical religious revival meetings in the Lebanon Valley, not far from Niskayuna.

Founding her humanitarian ideals on the French Camisard and Quaker movements, which had been developing in England at the time of her departure, Ann Lee enlarged on these philosophies and founded The United Society of Believers in Christ's Second Appearing. Their common name, Shakers, was derived from the fact that they shook and danced while praying as they attempted to purify and cast evil from themselves.

Visitors who came from New Lebanon were deeply moved by the Shakers' religious attitudes and beliefs. Slowly, the Shaker gospel converted people, who returned to their homes filled with love for the Shaker faith. These new Shaker converts helped to further spread the word of Mother Ann throughout

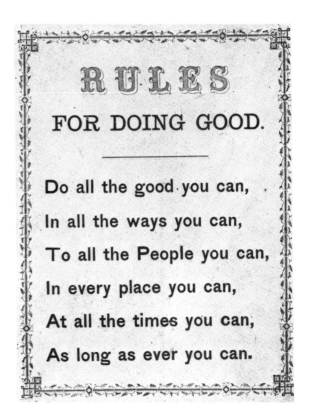

This broadside comes from the Mt. Lebanon, New York Shaker Village, circa 1882.

the New England states.

In 1784, The United Society finished building the first Shaker meeting house at New Lebanon. It was also in that year that Mother Ann died, leaving behind the growing roots of Shakerism.

Communities were formed in New Hampshire, Maine, and Massachusetts. In 1805, three Shaker brothers left for the Midwest to establish communities there. In the following decade, Shaker villages were firmly settled in South Union and Pleasant Hill, Kentucky as well as in Union Village, North Union, and Whitewater, Ohio. In all, nineteen communities were established.

The internal organization of these communities is interesting because all activities and work were communal. In addition, property was held in common. In all respects, men and women were separate but equal, and each member of the community was assumed to carry his share of responsibility with dignity.

The entire community was divided into groups called "families." They believed that they were all related to each other in just the same manner as blood-related brothers and sisters.

Each family had its own store, which was used as a clearinghouse for incoming and outgoing articles and products. If a family were affected by a natural misfortune, such as a fire or epidemic, other families or groups in the village would go to the aid of the victims.

Elders, who had been appointed by Mother Ann, were responsible for setting up and organizing the first Ministry. Trustees were appointed by the Ministry and Elders to handle all business dealings with non-Shakers or members of the outside world. The trustees were assisted by Deacons and Deaconesses who were responsible for the different trade shops and industries. The Shakers never let their religious zeal blind them to the fact that they had to get along and trade with the people around them to ensure their economic and financial survival.

So they began various business endeavors with the outside world. Fine craftsmanship, high quality, and honesty led to success and a reputation for integrity and fairness. What began as small ventures often developed into large-scale commercial enterprises.

Agriculture, of course, was the most important occupation. In 1790 the Shaker seed industry began; it lasted for more than a century. Broom corn was introduced and, consequently, Shaker brooms became a well-known product. The Shakers were also involved in collecting, growing and packaging herbs and herb medicines. They raised quality livestock and sheep, which in turn gave rise to a number of various trades, such as tanning and the manufacturing of fine flannel.

Different communities had their own regional specialities. Mt. Lebanon, New York produced thousands of commercial chairs and stools. South Union, Kentucky canned fruit. Shirley and Harvard, Massachusetts were leading producers of apple products, including cider, applesauce, and dried apples. Maple sap was harvested and refined into large quantities of maple sugar in New Hampshire. The Maine villages became known for their poplar-wood "fancy work" or sewing boxes and articles. The fur and wool hat business was concentrated in Han-

cock, Massachusetts as was the manufacture of wooden swifts, ingenious yarn-winding devices. North Union, Ohio thrived on business generated from grist and woolen mills. Pleasant Hill, Kentucky produced much cooperware (buckets, wash bowls, churns, and tubs) for sale. For example, 1,077 pieces of cooperware were sold in 1847. Their Elixir of Malt, selling at $1.00 a bottle, was also a popular product.

The Shakers' sole purpose in life was to establish God's kingdom on earth. Their minds, hearts, and hands were devoted to this ideal. "Hands to work and hearts to God" is a famous Shaker motto. So it is not surprising to see the emphasis on perfection that is inherent in their furniture's design and form. The absence of all ornaments, plush fabrics, and elaborately carved woods are just further evidence of this philosophy.

Beauty was not admired for its own sake. Only a non-Shaker could find any kind of

A Canterbury, New Hampshire Shaker sister, Rebecca Hathaway, weaving the taped seat of a Canterbury slat-back rocker.

solace or enlightenment in the appearance of an object. Aesthetics had no value, but craftsmanship certainly did. Lines were straight and simple. Functionalism and simplicity were inherent in Shaker design, not for lack of imagination, but because these elements were considered necessary in the search for the perfection of God's kingdom on earth. The Shaker faith was not just a religion, it was a way of life that greatly influenced everything the Shakers did and produced. In a Shaker periodical written in 1872, the writer asks, "What are goods worth unless they are full of genuine religion?"

The Shakers were always looking for the most practical and efficient timesaving devices and techniques. Their architecture and furniture reflected this search. Rooms had pegboards on walls so that chairs could easily be suspended to permit easy cleaning. There were no moldings or ornaments to catch dust. Many rooms contained large wall units and cupboards that supplied efficient and practical storage areas.

Shaker furniture was designed for utility. Long benches held numbers of people. Wood boxes had pegs to hold dustpans and brushes for easy availability. Inventive genius put rollers on beds so that they could be quickly moved for cleaning. A ball-and-socket device on the two rear legs of a chair allowed a person to "tilt" his chair after a hearty meal. These tilters or chair feet prevented the wear and tear of carpets and the marring of floors caused by the rear legs of the chair as it rocked back and forth.

The Shaker chair came in many variations but always kept a distinctive style. The majority of chairs were of straight, ladder-back form with three or four thin slats across the back, and two turned rungs on front and sides and one in back. The seat and, sometimes, the back were of woven tape or "webbed." The tops of the front posts were slightly rounded and the back posts were topped by graceful finials. So perfectly were Shaker chairs built that today there are many for sale by antique dealers who can offer them in fine condition after a century of good hard use.

Adherence to Shaker beliefs required not only separation from the world of non-Shakers, but also celibacy, the abstinence from what the Shakers referred to as "the sins of the flesh." Instructing that the absence of a physical relationship with the op-

This postcard shows the last of the Shaker sisters at Shaker Village, Harvard, Massachusetts, circa 1919.

posite sex as well as the absence of tangible material goods was the only way to reach a higher spiritual level of being, Shakerism was not an easy or casual religion. It was believed that by means of devotion to Shaker doctrine and diligent, consecrated labor, the foundation of Heaven would be established. The Shakers' daily activities of hard work in an environment of calm and order gave them a lasting, rich, and emotional fulfillment.

How then did they fail? Today, there are only nine living Shaker women, whereas in 1850, there had been some six thousand Shaker souls.

The most important factor in the Shakers' eventual decline was celibacy. Since they didn't believe in procreation, their very existence depended upon conversion of both adults and orphans to sustain their numbers. During the Civil War, there were no formal orphanages, and many families and friends of orphans brought them to live in Shaker communities where food, clothing, and work were in full supply. Although these orphans could choose to leave the Shaker village at age sixteen, many chose to remain. As the Industrial Age took hold and manufacturing led to job opportunities and affluence in the cities, many orphans chose to depart to find wealth and property in the outside world. Converts became fewer and fewer in number.

Eventually too, the original religious fervor wore down; revivals and fanatical sermons became a less meaningful part of the daily religious experience. Older Shakers were too infirm to maintain their former degree of enthusiasm and the younger ones were somehow less involved and less interested.

In a sense, Shakerism was a result of its times. The needs of the early nineteenth century reluctantly gave way to the industrial surge and big-city glitter. The agricultural foundations of American society dwindled away in the face of industrial development. The Shaker furniture maker, who carefully and painstakingly hand turned a chair piece, became an old-fashioned and expensive luxury. Factory-made furniture was cheaper and more available; thus, we can easily sense the inevitability of the Shaker decline.

But Shakerism is not dead. Its message will long be told, and Shaker design will most certainly endure. Those people who had the memorable ''gift to be a simple'' have left to us a rich and influential legacy, which only now is beginning to be fully appreciated.

Construction Supplies and Notes

Drafting Tools

Drafting tools are useful for carefully plotting out dimensions, taking accurate measurements, and making the kind of detailed measured drawings that are included in this book. These graphic artist's tools come in handy for a myriad of unexpected uses that inevitably crop up during the making of miniatures.

Protractor
T-square
30°-60°-90° triangle
45° triangle
Compass
Dividers
Single-edge razor blade
Eraser
Drafting pencil
Oval template
Circular template
Graph paper
Flexible rule
Masking tape
Tracing paper
Paper
Scotch tape
Scissors
Scale ruler

Woodworking Tools

Since cutting and joining are the basic operations of fine miniature making, you will need a number of cutting tools, mostly of miniature size. Many of these tools are carried by miniature outlets, hardware stores, and craft shops. Several outlets that carry many of the necessary supplies are listed in the Suppliers section.

Hand Tools

Sander
Hand drill and drill set
Coping saw
Spoke shave
Miter box
Razor saw
Knives, including X-acto knife with assorted
   blades
Jeweler's saw
Needle files
Vise
Mini-clamps
Round jeweler's file
Caliper
Miniature screwdrivers
Miniature turning tools
Small chisel
Hand drill
Keyhole saw
Hand saber saw
Center punches

Moto-Lathe (important for perfectly turned wood)
Moto-Tool and drill press stand (a basic tool for just about every operation in miniature furniture production)
Moto-Saw

Miscellaneous

Magnifier
Tweezers
Toothpicks
Elmer's Glue-All
Slomon's Sobo Glue

Notes on Making Shaker Miniature Furniture

All miniature furniture in this book is in the scale of one inch equals one foot. The measurements in the line drawings are all listed in inches.

After all the pieces are cut to size, drilled, and sanded, stain each piece. Staining before gluing ensures even penetration of the stain. Where glue seeps from a joint, the wood becomes sealed and will not take stain.

For all staining, we recommend wood finishes by Minwax; these are easy to apply and available in fifteen natural colors. Carver Tripp's wood stain is also good. Both penetrate the wood with one coat and seal it with a hard, protective finish. For painted pieces, such as the red blanket chest or the green bed, we recommend a flat paint or a Shaker-inspired paint available from the Guild of Shaker Crafts, 401 West Savidge Street, Spring Lake, Michigan 4956. The Guild also produces Shaker-inspired finishes and will send samples on request. A catalog is available for $2.50 postpaid.

Sanding should be done intermittently through the various stages of furniture construction in order to refine the wood surface. Sand lightly using fine sandpaper or a sander. Always sand flat surfaces with a straight motion following the grain of the wood. Circular motions or sanding against the grain will mar the surface of the wood.

For the bent curves in many pieces, bend the wood by soaking it in warm to hot water for a few hours or overnight if necessary. Be sure that the piece of wood is weighted down so that it is immersed and will absorb the water. Remove the wood from the water, wrap it around a mold of the particular curve you need, and hold it in place with clamps. Allow the wood to dry overnight. When completely dry, sand, stain, and assemble the piece.

Scoring means to groove part-way into a solid surface. This can be done with a knife or, as in the case of the miniature room's floor, with a dull pencil to give the effect of planks.

Community Dining Table

Since eating meals was a communal experience, dining tables had to be long and accommodating. Ten- and twenty-foot tables were not uncommon. Trestle dining tables were the most frequent design. They consisted of a four-board top with breadboard ends, which prevented warping, and were supported by two or three pedestal legs or trestles.

The Shakers ate their meals in silence with men and women seated at separate tables. There was always plenty of fruit and dairy products, including eggs and cheese, on the table. In many communities neither tea nor coffee was served.

To facilitate the passing of dishes, dining tables were set to fit one or more "squares" of four persons each. Thus, a ten-foot table served three squares; a twenty-foot table could hold up to twenty people.

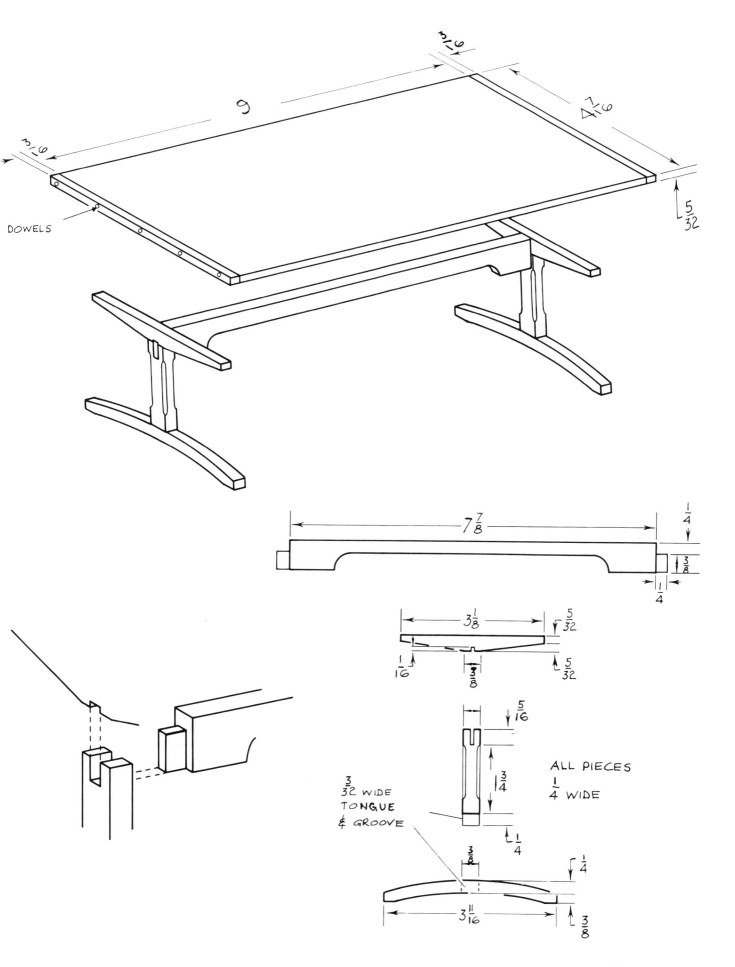

DOWELS

$\frac{3}{16}$

6

$4\frac{7}{16}$

$\frac{3}{16}$

$\frac{5}{32}$

$7\frac{7}{8}$

$\frac{1}{4}$

$\frac{3}{8}$

$\frac{1}{4}$

$3\frac{1}{8}$

$\frac{5}{32}$

$\frac{1}{16}$

$\frac{3}{8}$

$\frac{5}{32}$

$\frac{5}{16}$

$1\frac{3}{4}$

$\frac{1}{4}$

ALL PIECES $\frac{1}{4}$ WIDE

$\frac{3}{32}$ WIDE
TONGUE
& GROOVE

$\frac{3}{8}$

$\frac{1}{4}$

$3\frac{11}{16}$

$\frac{3}{8}$

Dining Chair

The backs of Shaker dining chairs were low so that they could be pushed under the table or hung on a pegboard for efficient cleaning and easy storage. The two-slat type replaced an earlier one-slat chair that provided insufficient back support.

These chairs were commonly of maple and were produced with only small variations in design in many Shaker communities. They are a perfect example of how an article of furniture can be perfectly suited to its need.

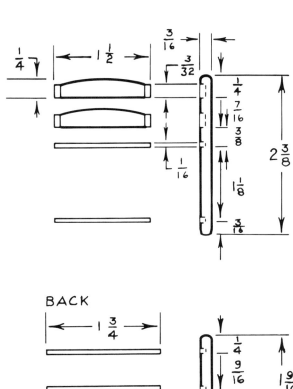

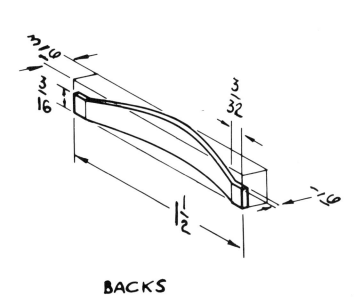

BACKS

BACK

FRONT

SIDES

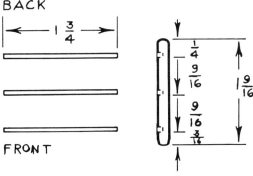

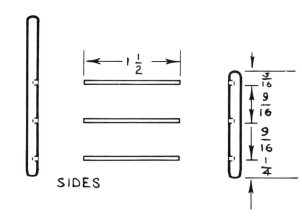

21

Ministry's Dining Table

The Ministry's dining table is similar to the community's but is shorter and more compact. The Ministry, considered a higher rank of Shaker society and composed of two elders and two eldresses, ate apart from the rest of the people in the community. Since all tables made for use in the community were custom produced for a special purpose, it can be said that particular care would be taken for an item for the Ministry's own use. Some tables were entirely made of cherry or walnut, giving a very handsome appearance.

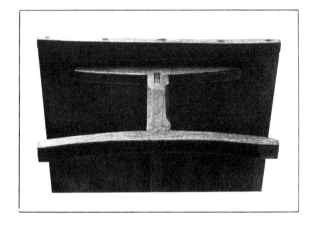

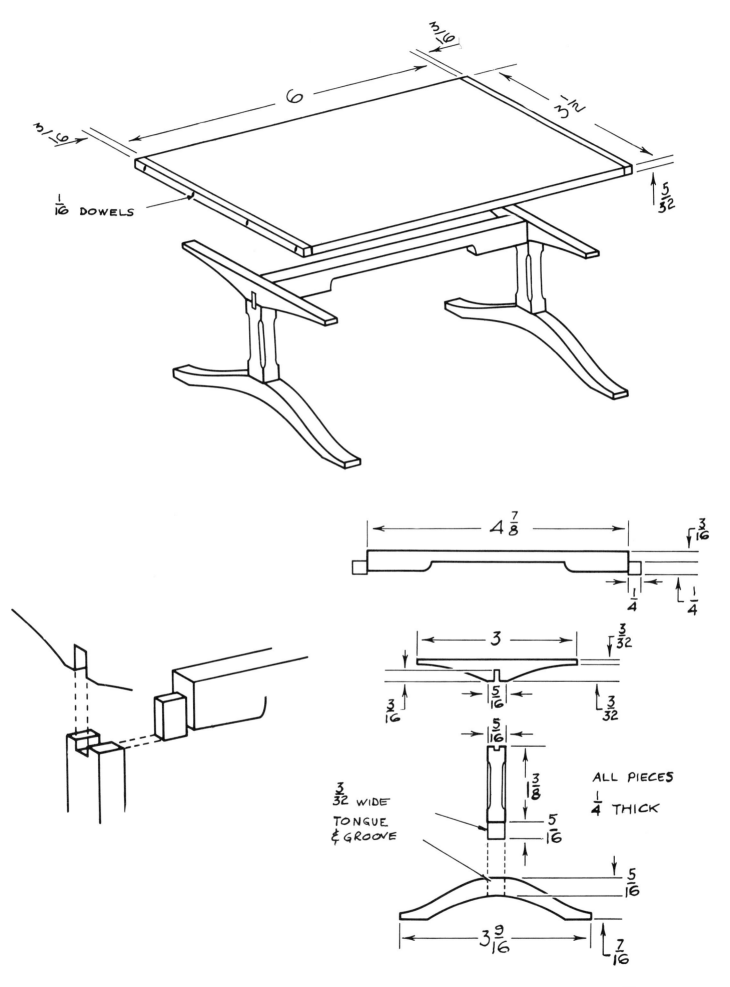

$\frac{3}{16}$

6

$3\frac{1}{2}$

$\frac{3}{16}$

$\frac{5}{32}$

$\frac{1}{16}$ DOWELS

$4\frac{7}{8}$

$\frac{3}{16}$

$\frac{1}{4}$

$\frac{1}{4}$

3

$\frac{3}{32}$

$\frac{3}{16}$

$\frac{5}{16}$

$\frac{3}{32}$

$\frac{5}{16}$

$\frac{3}{8}$

$1\frac{3}{8}$

ALL PIECES

$\frac{1}{4}$ THICK

$\frac{3}{32}$ WIDE

TONGUE & GROOVE

$\frac{5}{16}$

$\frac{5}{16}$

$\frac{5}{16}$

$3\frac{9}{16}$

$\frac{7}{16}$

Ministry's Side Chair

Although the Shakers did not invent the ladderback chair, they did much to adapt the Colonial form to their own requirements. Here for the Ministry's dining needs, we find a chair, which is very simple and strong, and yet is of entirely different appearance from the remainder of the community's dining chairs. We can only guess that its taller form indicates a more important service.

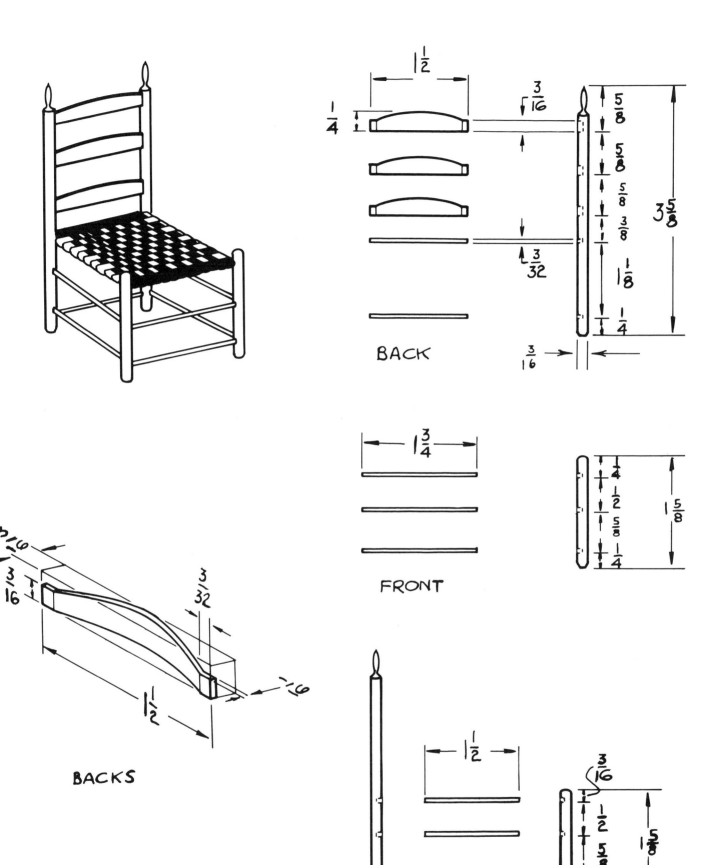

BACK

FRONT

BACKS

SIDES

Settee

The Shaker settee had a slab seat, four turned legs, and an elegant row of spindles, which are slightly bent. Other models had straight spindles. Noteworthy is the lack of long, back and front stretchers. This absence tended to give a more graceful appearance to the Shaker design compared to its world counterpart, but probably made it more unstable as well.

This miniature is fashioned after an Enfield, New Hampshire settee; however, both Canterbury, New Hampshire and Harvard, Massachusetts also have been credited with the origin of this form.

Designs as well as inventions spread from one community to another so it is not difficult to understand how a design's origin could be lost to all historians.

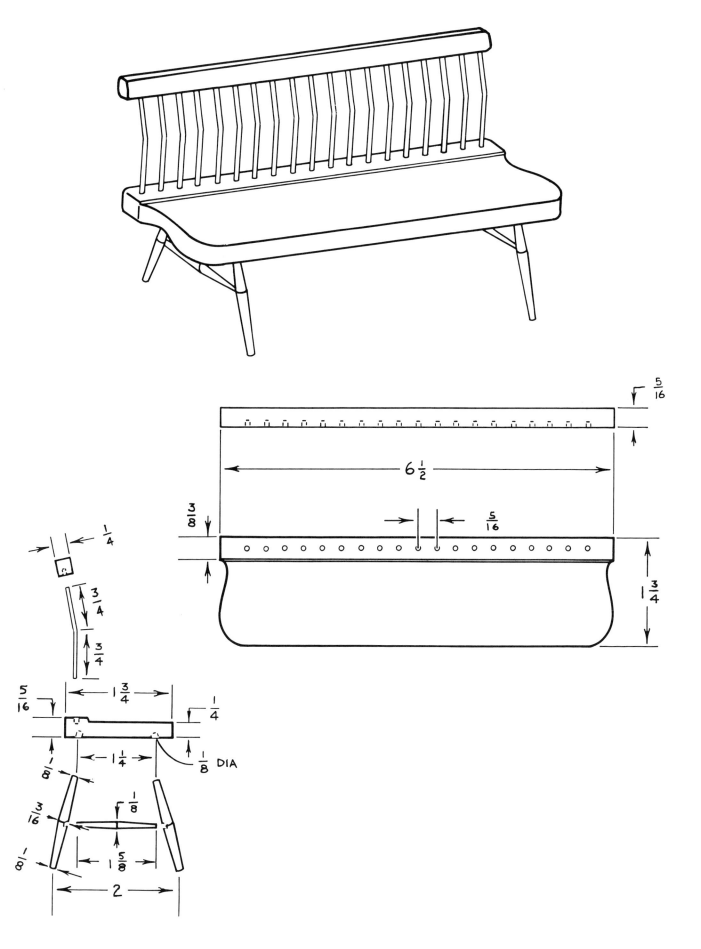

$\frac{5}{16}$

$6\frac{1}{2}$

$\frac{3}{8}$

$\frac{5}{16}$

$1\frac{3}{4}$

$\frac{1}{4}$

$\frac{3}{4}$

$\frac{3}{4}$

$\frac{5}{16}$

$1\frac{3}{4}$

$\frac{1}{4}$

$1\frac{1}{4}$

$\frac{1}{8}$ DIA

$\frac{1}{8}$

$\frac{3}{16}$

$\frac{1}{8}$

$1\frac{5}{8}$

$\frac{1}{8}$

2

Web-back Rocker

Probably the most well-known example of Shaker furniture is the Shaker rocker. Ever since the 1870s when the commercial chair business was pursued in earnest, the Shaker rocker was a noted and popular product. The Shakers were probably the first commercial manufacturer of chairs, and probably the first commercially to produce rockers for sale.

The seat and back of this chair are made from worsted tape, also called webbing or "listing." At first, all tape was woven by the sisters on their own tape looms, but later a commercial tape was purchased and considered more economical. These tapes were woven into many different color combinations or patterns bringing a touch of color to the natural wood or dark finish of the rocker frame.

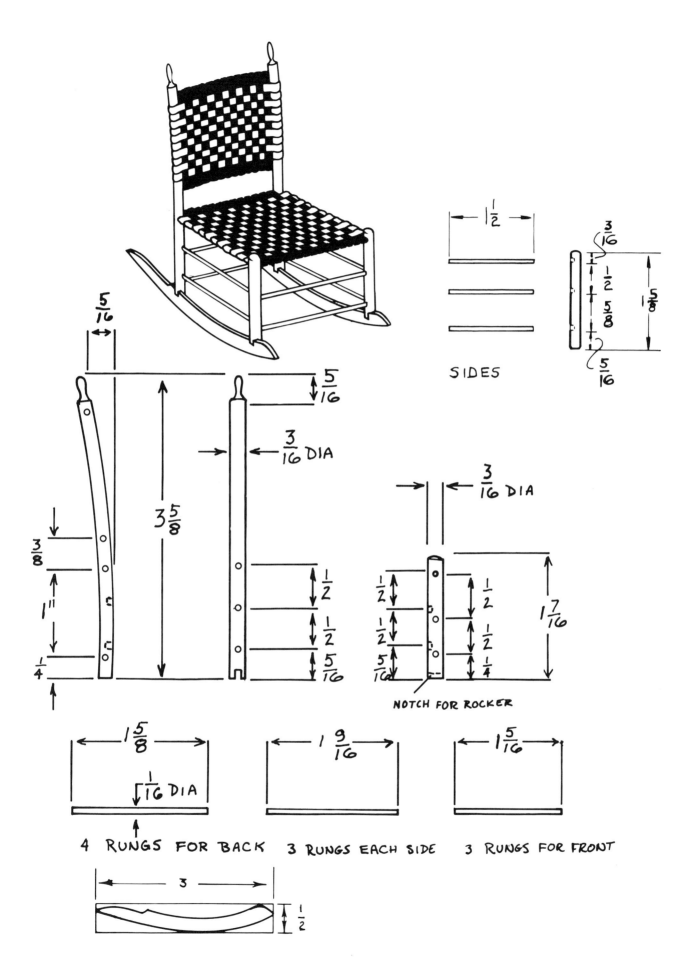

$\frac{1}{2}$

SIDES

$\frac{3}{16}$

$\frac{1}{2}$

$\frac{5}{8}$

$\frac{5}{16}$

$1\frac{5}{8}$

$\frac{5}{16}$

$\frac{5}{16}$

$\frac{3}{16}$ DIA

$3\frac{5}{8}$

$\frac{3}{8}$

$1''$

$\frac{1}{4}$

$\frac{1}{2}$

$\frac{1}{2}$

$\frac{5}{16}$

$\frac{3}{16}$ DIA

$\frac{1}{2}$

$\frac{1}{2}$

$\frac{5}{16}$

$\frac{1}{2}$

$\frac{1}{2}$

$\frac{1}{4}$

$1\frac{7}{16}$

NOTCH FOR ROCKER

$1\frac{5}{8}$

$\frac{1}{16}$ DIA

4 RUNGS FOR BACK

$1\frac{9}{16}$

3 RUNGS EACH SIDE

$1\frac{5}{16}$

3 RUNGS FOR FRONT

3

$\frac{1}{2}$

Slat-back Rocker with Arms

Although the Shakers were known to have used cane, splint, and rush seats, it is certain that their favorite material was woven tape, also called braid, worsted lace, and "listing." When the Shakers started to buy this "outside," they first purchased commercially manufactured woolen worsted and later, a cotton canvas. It wore well and, provided that the seats were stuffed properly, didn't sag or give way. In reading a Shaker chair catalog, purchasers of this chair would be offered a choice of one or two colors in combination from a total of fourteen colors, including light blue, peacock blue, pomegranate, grass green, old gold, drab, and orange.

Unlike other chairs of the period, Shaker chairs were light, yet strong and proved very good commercial items.

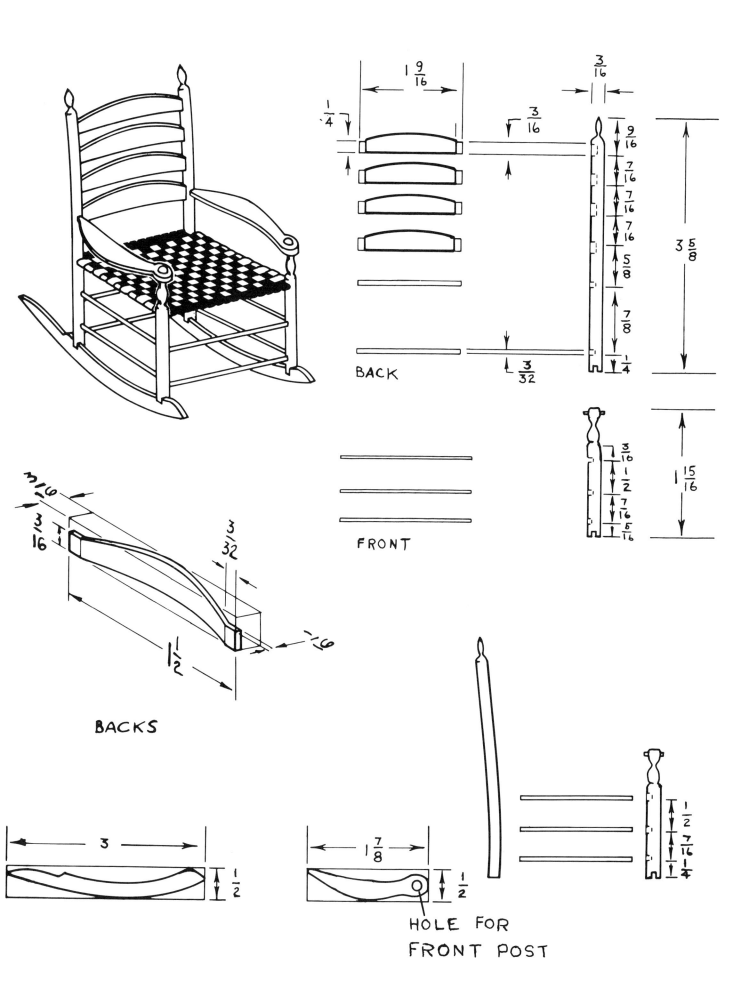

$1\frac{9}{16}$

$\frac{3}{16}$

$\frac{1}{4}$

$\frac{3}{16}$

$\frac{9}{16}$

$\frac{7}{16}$

$\frac{7}{16}$

$\frac{7}{16}$

$\frac{5}{8}$

$3\frac{5}{8}$

$\frac{7}{8}$

BACK

$\frac{3}{32}$

$\frac{1}{4}$

$\frac{3}{16}$

$\frac{1}{2}$

$\frac{7}{16}$

$\frac{5}{16}$

$1\frac{15}{16}$

FRONT

$\frac{3}{16}$

$\frac{3}{16}$

$\frac{3}{32}$

$\frac{1}{16}$

$1\frac{1}{2}$

BACKS

3

$\frac{1}{2}$

$1\frac{7}{8}$

$\frac{1}{2}$

HOLE FOR
FRONT POST

$\frac{1}{2}$

$\frac{7}{16}$

$\frac{1}{4}$

Bar-slat-back Rocker

This unique chair is commonly called a "shawl-back" or "shawl-rail" rocker. The tradition is that a Shaker sister could rest comfortably by placing her shawl behind her suspended from the upper bar or rail. However, original chair catalogs clearly state that "the bars across the top of the back posts are intended for cushions, but will be furnished to order without additional cost." To this bar would be attached a durable "heavy wool plush" cushion, that could come in one of many colors, or else have a different color border with colored stripes. Thus, contrary to common belief, we discover that the main use of the upper bar would be to attach a plush cushion.

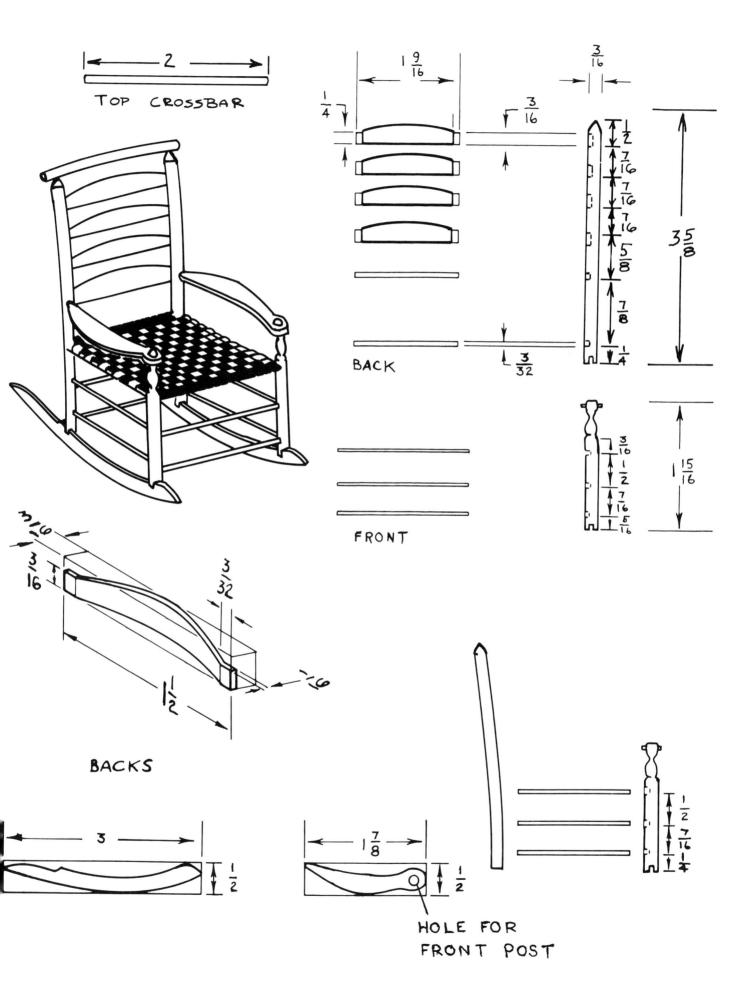

TOP CROSSBAR

2

BACK

1 9/16   3/16   3/16

1/4   3/16   3/32

1/2
7/16
7/16
7/16
5/8
7/8
1/4

35 5/8

1 15/16

3/16
1/2
7/16
5/16

FRONT

BACKS

3/16
3/16
3/32
1/6
1 1/2

3
1/2

1 7/8
1/2

HOLE FOR
FRONT POST

1/2
7/16
1/4

Slat-back Rocker

As was noted earlier, the most important requisite of the Shaker chair was function. To be perfectly useful, the article had to be exactly suited to its need. A chair must be strong; it must be light and durable.

Chairs and rockers reflect the grace and simplicity associated with all things Shaker. One of the more distinguishing characteristics is the delicate finial at the top of each back post. Although these often displayed regional and even community characteristics, they were always in harmony with the chair frame.

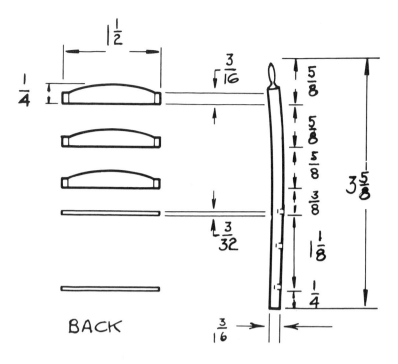

$1\frac{1}{2}$

$\frac{3}{16}$

$\frac{1}{4}$

$\frac{5}{8}$

$\frac{5}{8}$

$\frac{5}{8}$

$\frac{3}{8}$

$3\frac{5}{8}$

$\frac{3}{32}$

$1\frac{1}{8}$

$\frac{1}{4}$

$\frac{3}{16}$

BACK

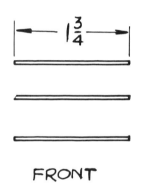

$1\frac{3}{4}$

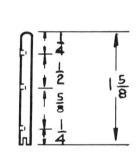

$\frac{1}{4}$

$\frac{1}{2}$

$\frac{5}{8}$

$\frac{1}{4}$

$1\frac{5}{8}$

FRONT

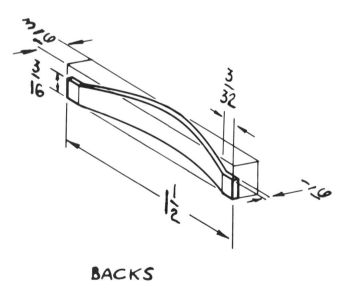

$\frac{3}{16}$

$\frac{3}{16}$

$\frac{3}{32}$

$\frac{1}{16}$

$1\frac{1}{2}$

BACKS

3

$\frac{1}{2}$

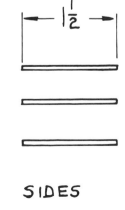

$1\frac{1}{2}$

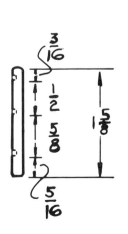

$\frac{3}{16}$

$\frac{1}{2}$

$\frac{5}{8}$

$1\frac{5}{8}$

$\frac{5}{16}$

SIDES

Spindle-back Rocker

The spindle-back rocker was an unusual Shaker design. Although it has not been found in any original Shaker catalog, it is said to have been produced at Mt. Lebanon, New York around 1875. Often it is called a Brother Gregory Chair, but we can find no reason for it being called this. All research has failed to find any Brother Gregory involved with the chair industry.

However, this particular design has been much imitated over the years by many chair factories and thus a number of inferior-quality imitations can be readily seen at flea markets and antique shows. With all the information coming to light on Shaker topics and furniture, it is interesting to note that there are still a few mysteries left.

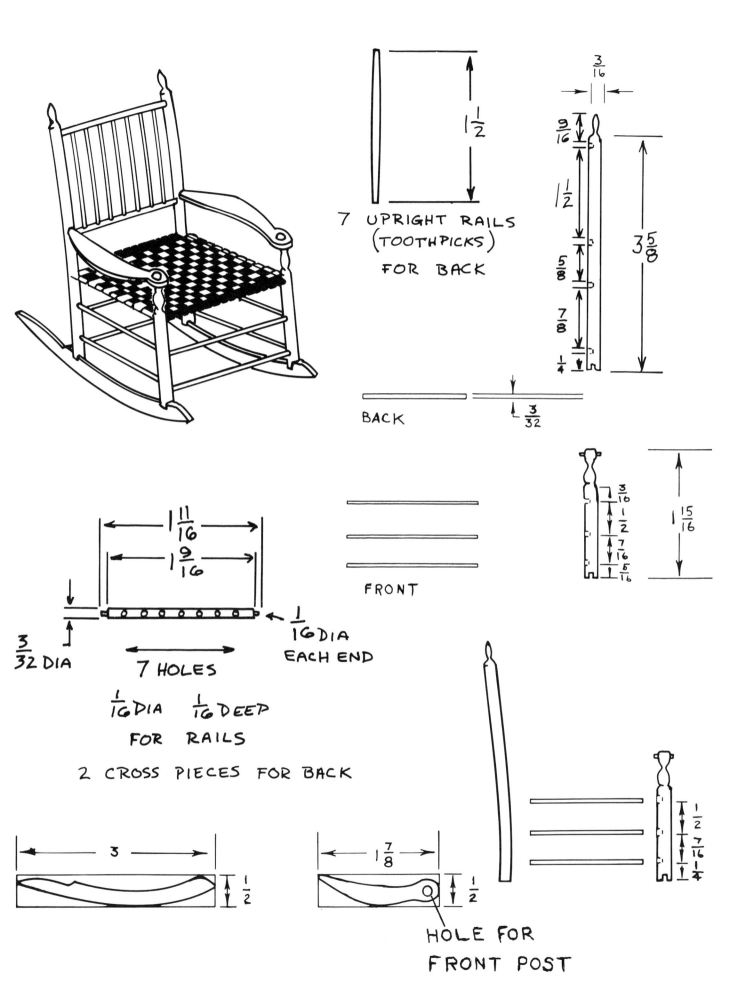

7 UPRIGHT RAILS
(TOOTHPICKS)
FOR BACK

$\frac{3}{16}$

$\frac{9}{16}$

$1\frac{1}{2}$

$\frac{5}{8}$

$\frac{7}{8}$

$\frac{1}{4}$

$3\frac{5}{8}$

BACK

$\frac{3}{32}$

$\frac{3}{16}$

$\frac{1}{2}$

$\frac{7}{16}$

$\frac{5}{16}$

$1\frac{15}{16}$

FRONT

$1\frac{11}{16}$

$1\frac{9}{16}$

$\frac{3}{32}$ DIA

$\frac{1}{16}$ DIA
EACH END

7 HOLES

$\frac{1}{16}$ DIA $\frac{1}{16}$ DEEP
FOR RAILS

2 CROSS PIECES FOR BACK

3

$\frac{1}{2}$

$1\frac{7}{8}$

$\frac{1}{2}$

HOLE FOR
FRONT POST

$1\frac{1}{2}$

$\frac{7}{16}$

$\frac{1}{4}$

Tilting Chair

The most innovative feature of a number of Shaker chairs were tilters or ball-and-socket devices. These were wooden balls fitted into a socket at the base of the rear chair legs and joined by a leather thong knotted at the base of the ball. This thong passed through a hole in the ball and through another hole in the leg. It rested flat on the floor. This device allowed one to lean back comfortably without damaging carpets or floors. In 1852, George O. Donnell patented a metal version of this device, which he called "chair feet."

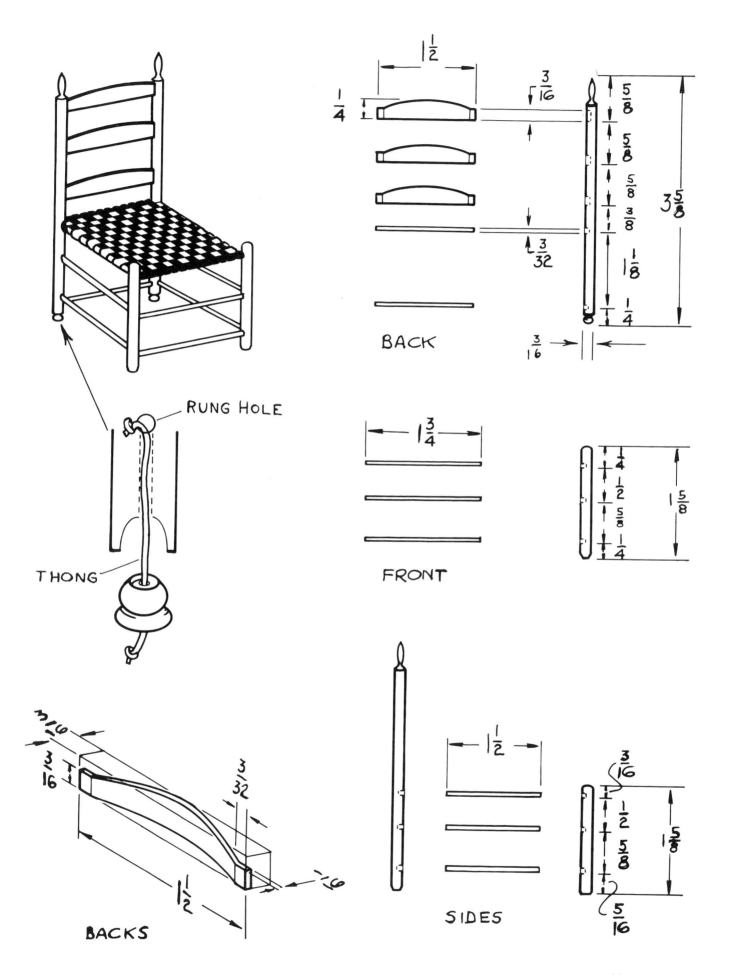

RUNG HOLE

THONG

BACK

FRONT

SIDES

BACKS

Clock

The clock was never a common piece of Shaker furniture. At first, clocks were only used in halls and were always simple items devoid of all decoration, but according to the June 1887 issue of *The Manifesto* (a monthly Shaker publication published in Canterbury, New Hampshire from 1884–1889) "The clock is an emblem of a Shaker community. . . . Promptness, absolute punctuality, is a *sine qua non* (indispensable thing) of a successful community."

According to Robert Meader, Director Emeritus of the Shaker Museum in Old Chatham, New York, there were nine Shaker clockmakers, two of whom left the Shaker faith. The Youngs family from Connecticut was responsible for three clockmakers, Benjamin, a founder of the Watervliet, New York community; his nephew, Benjamin Seth; and Isaac Newton Youngs, brother of Benjamin Seth. The first documented Shaker clockmaker was Amos Jewett of Mt. Lebanon, New York, who lived from 1753 to 1834.

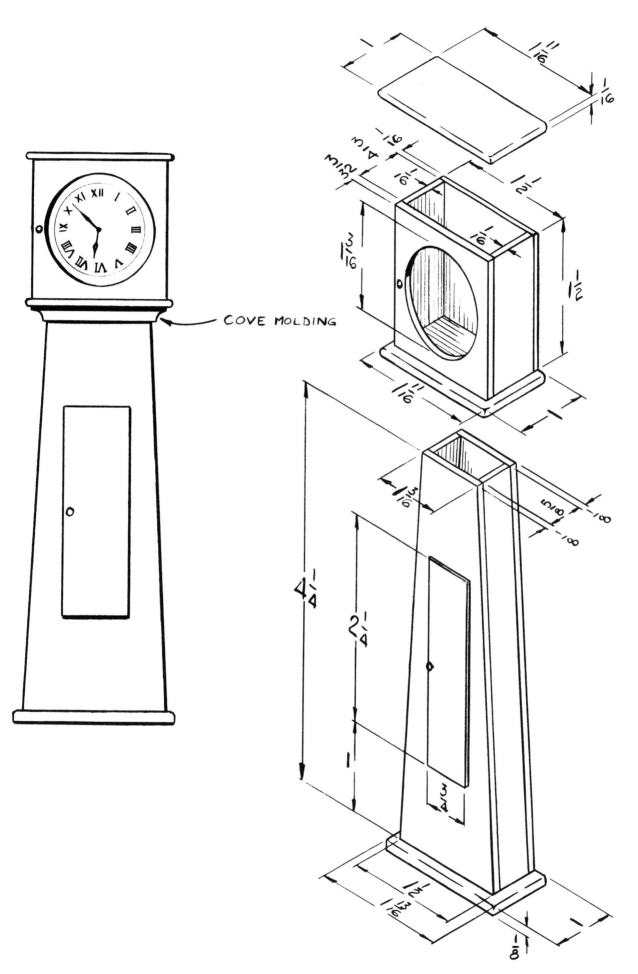

COVE MOLDING

Wall Clock

Of course, the wall clock must hang from a Shaker peg! The backboard is extended at the top to allow for a hole which lets the clock be hung from the pegboard. Isaac Newton Youngs of New Lebanon, New York is known to have made a number of wall clocks; two such clocks can be viewed at Hancock Shaker Village in Massachusetts. As seemingly exceptions to the rule, clockmakers were allowed to sign their work so we are able to identify particular clockmakers by name.

The simplicity of Shaker clock design is yet another example of their relationship between religion and form. On the antique market, Shaker clocks are considered one of the most expensive Shaker artifacts.

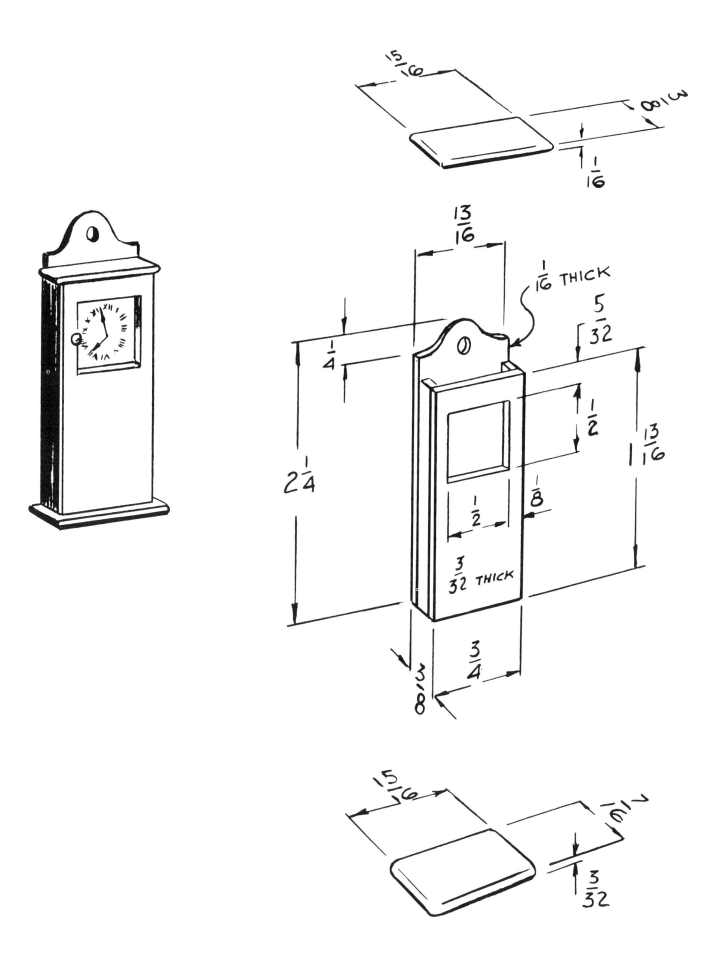

$\frac{15}{16}$

$\frac{3}{8}$

$\frac{1}{16}$

$\frac{13}{16}$

$\frac{1}{16}$ THICK

$\frac{5}{32}$

$\frac{1}{4}$

$\frac{1}{2}$

$\frac{13}{16}$

$2\frac{1}{4}$

$\frac{1}{2}$

$\frac{1}{8}$

$\frac{3}{32}$ THICK

$\frac{3}{8}$

$\frac{3}{4}$

$\frac{15}{16}$

$\frac{1}{16}$

$\frac{3}{32}$

43

Washstand

The importance of personal cleanliness was paramount in Shaker philosophy. The washstand is by no means a unique Shaker design, but it was a necessary article of furniture at a time when there was no running hot and cold water. Its function, simplicity, and good craftsmanship in fine, seasoned woods describe a piece that was fashioned with patience and love. There was a washstand either in every bedroom or in a small room connected directly to the bedroom.

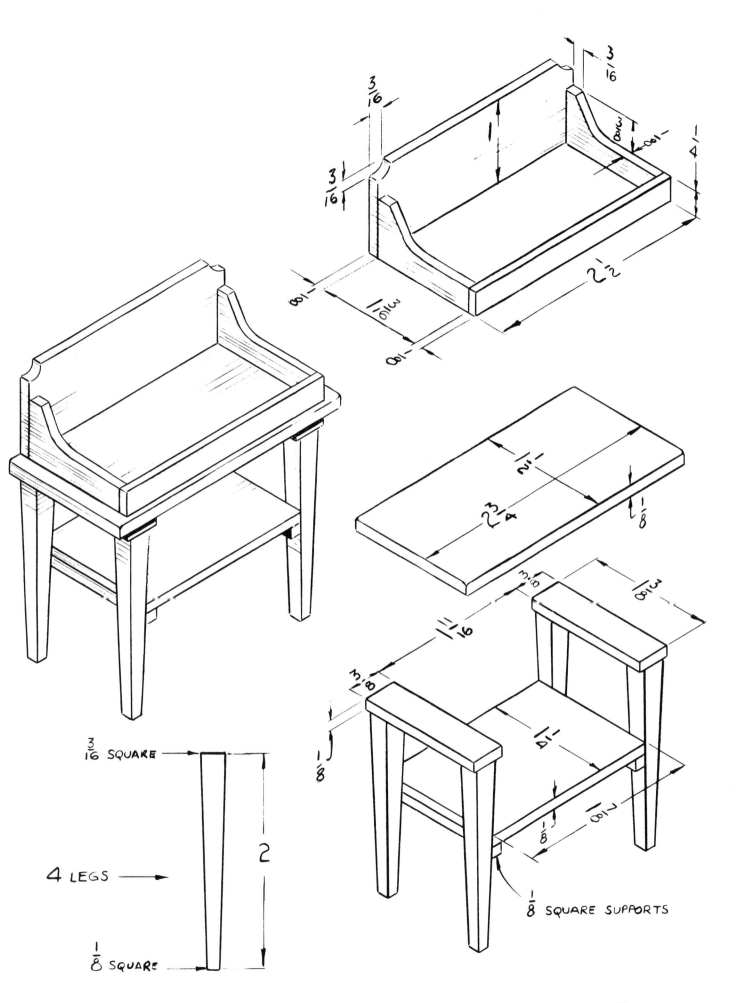

$\frac{3}{16}$

$\frac{3}{16}$

$\frac{3}{16}$

$\frac{3}{16}$

1

$\frac{3}{8}$

$\frac{1}{8}$

$1\frac{1}{4}$

$2\frac{1}{2}$

$\frac{1}{8}$

$\frac{3}{16}$

$\frac{1}{8}$

$2\frac{1}{2}$

$2\frac{3}{4}$

$\frac{1}{8}$

$\frac{3}{8}$

$\frac{3}{8}$

$1\frac{1}{16}$

$\frac{3}{8}$

$1\frac{1}{4}$

$\frac{1}{8}$

$\frac{2}{8}$

$\frac{1}{8}$

$\frac{3}{16}$ SQUARE

2

4 LEGS

$\frac{1}{8}$ SQUARE

$\frac{1}{8}$ SQUARE SUPPORTS

45

Work Table

For the most part, Shaker tables were not sold outside the different communities. They were designed for the Shakers own use and, today, we can see countless varieties in all sizes and shapes. This table, with its long tapered legs, is interesting because of its false drawer front. We cannot identify a special function for it, but its graceful design is a pleasant addition to any room.

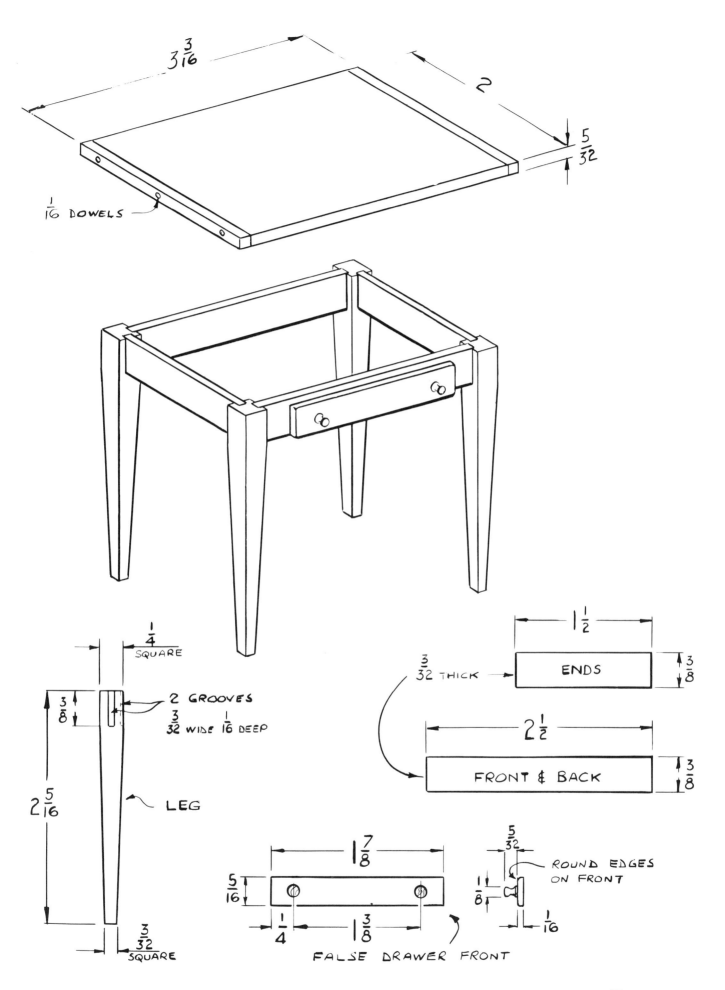

$3\frac{3}{16}$

2

$\frac{5}{32}$

$\frac{1}{16}$ DOWELS

$\frac{1}{4}$ SQUARE

$\frac{3}{8}$

2 GROOVES
$\frac{3}{32}$ WIDE $\frac{1}{16}$ DEEP

$2\frac{5}{16}$

LEG

$\frac{3}{32}$ SQUARE

$1\frac{1}{2}$

ENDS

$\frac{3}{32}$ THICK

$\frac{3}{8}$

$2\frac{1}{2}$

FRONT & BACK

$\frac{3}{8}$

$1\frac{7}{8}$

$\frac{5}{16}$

$\frac{1}{4}$ $\frac{3}{8}$

$\frac{5}{32}$

$\frac{1}{8}$

ROUND EDGES
ON FRONT

$\frac{1}{16}$

FALSE DRAWER FRONT

Ironing Table

The ironing table is of the X-trestle style with breadboard ends and long horizontal stretchers. This was a type of table used for many purposes in the community—in storerooms, kitchens, and work areas. Larger tables of this style were also produced for certain tasks, such as canning and apple-sorting. Ironing, however, was a most important chore in a community that included many people and in which there were always a lot of clothes to wash and iron.

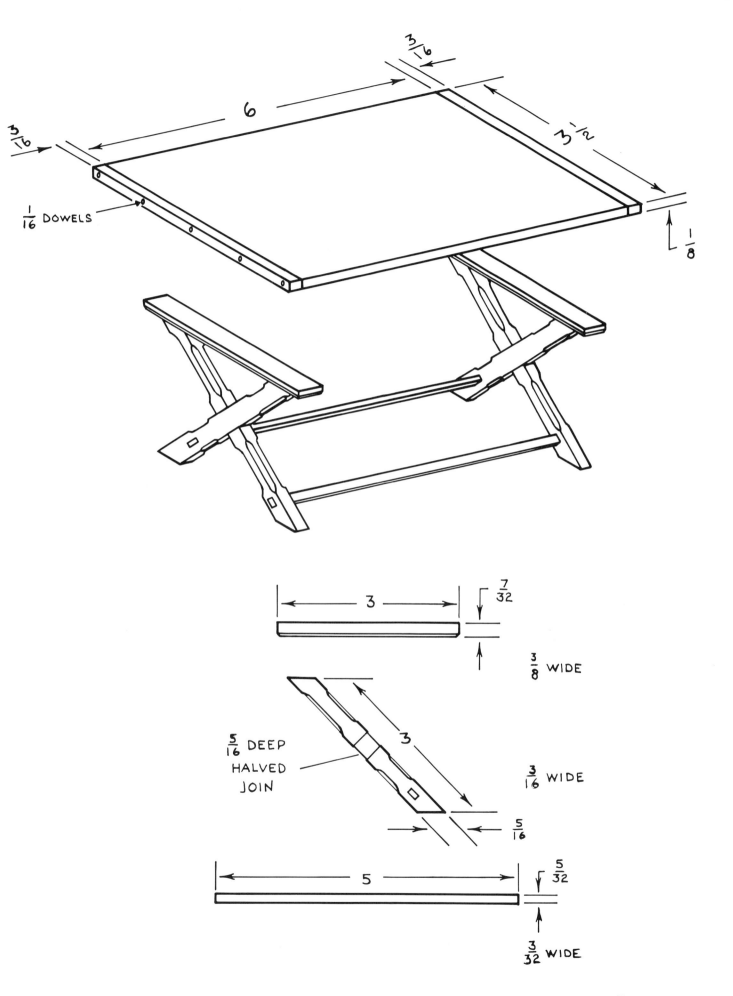

$\frac{3}{16}$

6

$\frac{3}{16}$

$3\frac{1}{2}$

$\frac{1}{8}$

$\frac{1}{16}$ DOWELS

$\frac{7}{32}$

3

$\frac{3}{8}$ WIDE

$\frac{5}{16}$ DEEP
HALVED
JOIN

3

$\frac{3}{16}$ WIDE

$\frac{5}{16}$

$\frac{5}{32}$

5

$\frac{3}{32}$ WIDE

Ironing Chair

In a communal village such as the Shakers', one can easily understand the need for specific pieces of furniture for particular work. Ironing was no exception. Many kinds of chairs for specific work for different people were made for domestic use. Since the sisters used a rotating system of work, often the same type of chair had to be made with different measurements to fit individual people. Chairs of this type were used in variations for work at desks, counters, and in the laundry.

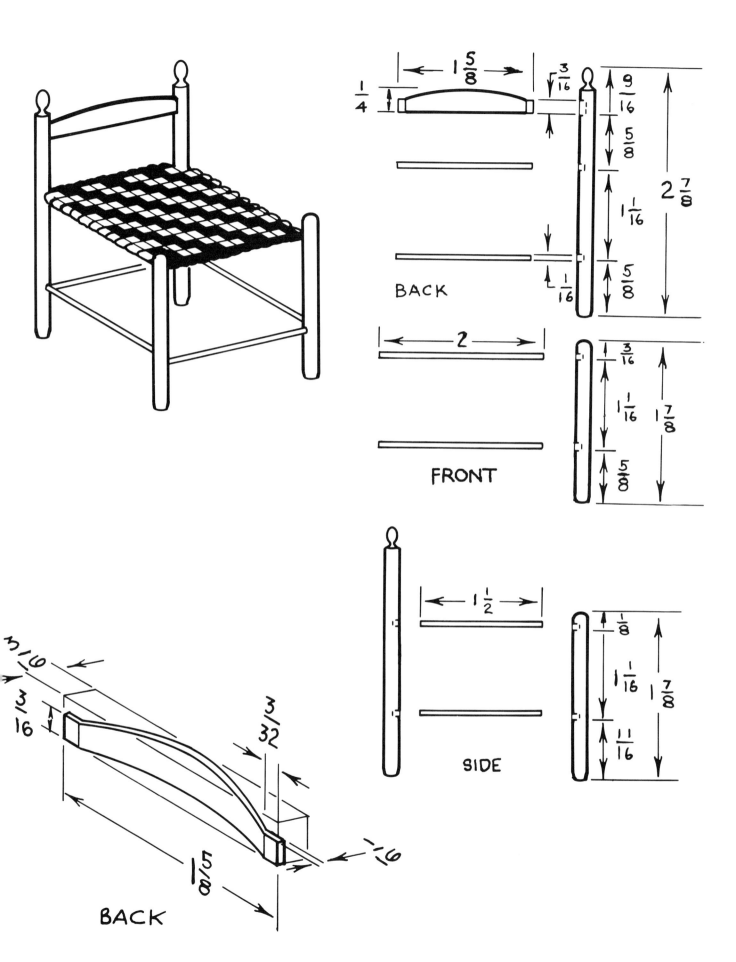

BACK

FRONT

SIDE

BACK

Tripod Workstand

According to Edward Deming and Faith Andrews in their book, *Shaker Furniture,* tripod workstands with spacious tops were uncommon items of Shaker craftsmanship. Their tops and drawers were usually made of pine; the pedestals and feet, of maple or some other hardwood. Earlier types with straight legs or ''peg legs'' were being made in New Lebanon, New York as early as 1805. This particular piece with its rounded or curved feet was a later one.

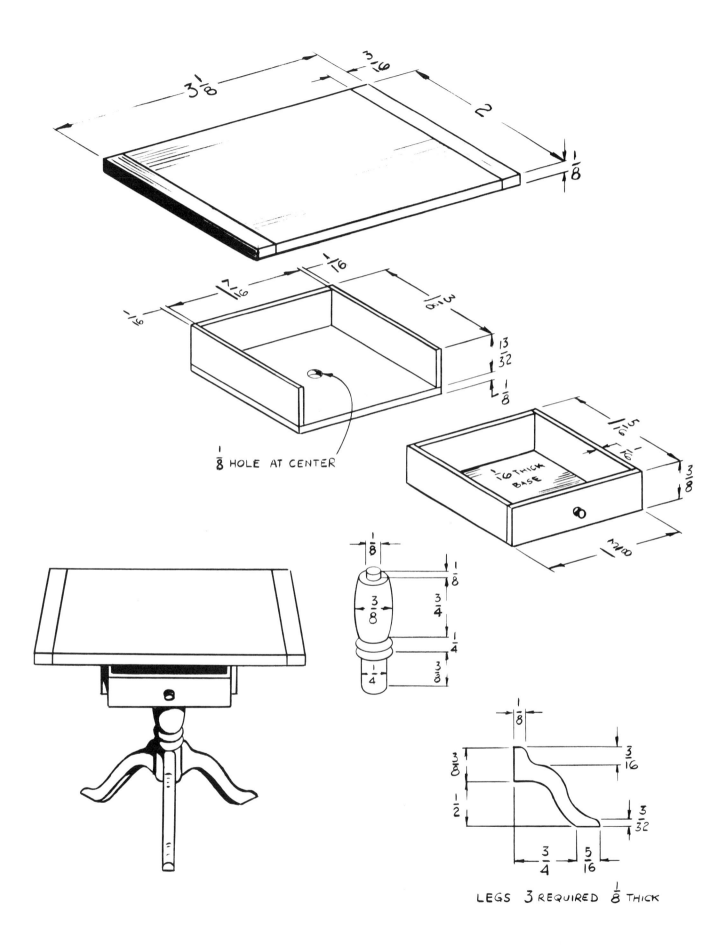

$3\frac{1}{8}$

$\frac{3}{16}$

2

$\frac{1}{8}$

$\frac{1}{16}$

$2\frac{7}{16}$

$\frac{1}{16}$

$3\frac{1}{8}$

$\frac{13}{32}$

$\frac{1}{8}$

$\frac{1}{8}$ HOLE AT CENTER

$3\frac{5}{16}$

$\frac{1}{16}$

$\frac{1}{16}$ THICK BASE

$3\frac{3}{8}$

$1\frac{3}{8}$

$\frac{1}{8}$

$\frac{1}{8}$

$\frac{3}{8}$

$\frac{3}{4}$

$\frac{1}{4}$

$\frac{3}{8}$

$\frac{1}{4}$

$\frac{1}{8}$

$3\frac{3}{8}$

$1\frac{1}{2}$

$\frac{3}{16}$

$\frac{3}{32}$

$\frac{3}{4}$

$\frac{5}{16}$

LEGS 3 REQUIRED $\frac{1}{8}$ THICK

Candlestand

Candlestands, generally of maple and cherry, were made in all Shaker communities. Although they were built in a variety of styles, this particular type is considered the most typical.

This round, graceful, and functional design graced just about every Shaker bedroom, and its arched legs became known as "spider legs." These stands were recognized for their beautiful proportions and balance. A candle, as well as many other small artifacts, could easily sit on its top.

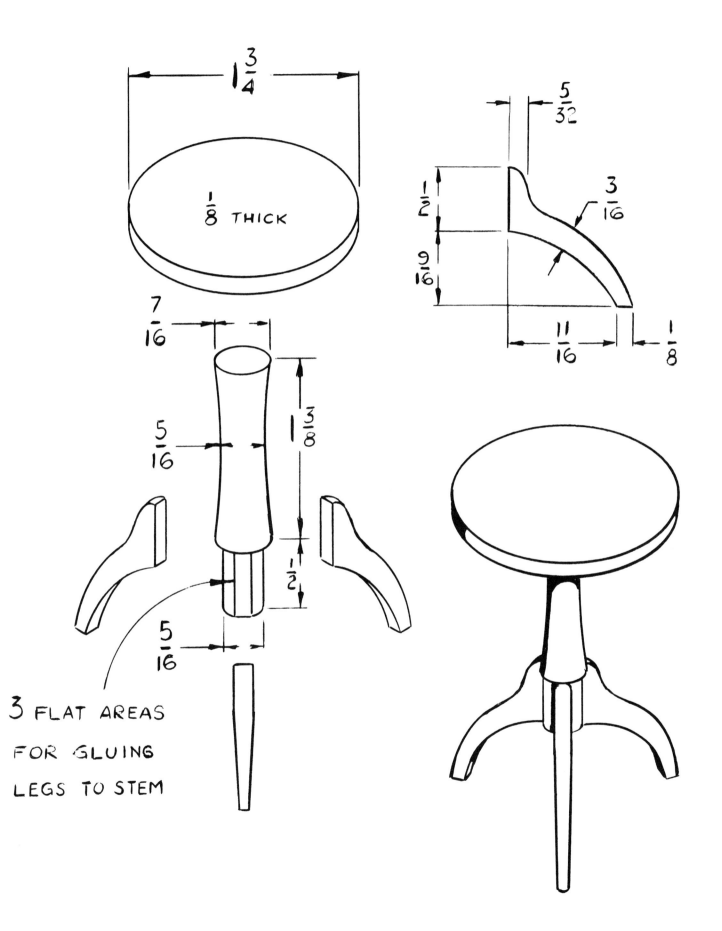

$1\frac{3}{4}$

$\frac{1}{8}$ THICK

$\frac{5}{32}$

$1\frac{1}{2}$

$\frac{9}{16}$

$\frac{3}{16}$

$\frac{11}{16}$

$\frac{1}{8}$

$\frac{7}{16}$

$\frac{5}{16}$

$1\frac{3}{8}$

$\frac{1}{2}$

$\frac{5}{16}$

3 FLAT AREAS
FOR GLUING
LEGS TO STEM

Bed

The Shaker bed was a simple one. Its purpose was to provide a place for sleeping and nothing else. In accordance with Shaker laws, originally all beds were painted green; however, later they were no longer painted. The Shakers called their beds "bed-steads," and to us they would seem more like narrow cots.

Usually, the top posts were plain as were the legs. The mattress platform was webbed with rope. This old-fashioned version of the bed spring was covered with a corn-husk-filled mattress. The bottoms of the legs were fitted with either wooden or cast-iron wheels or casters so the bed could be moved around for easy and efficient cleaning.

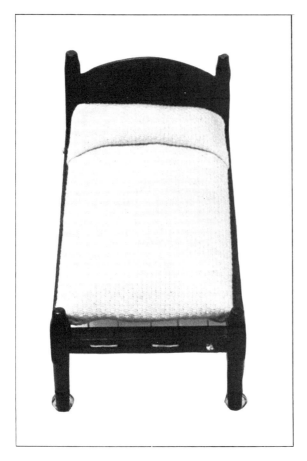

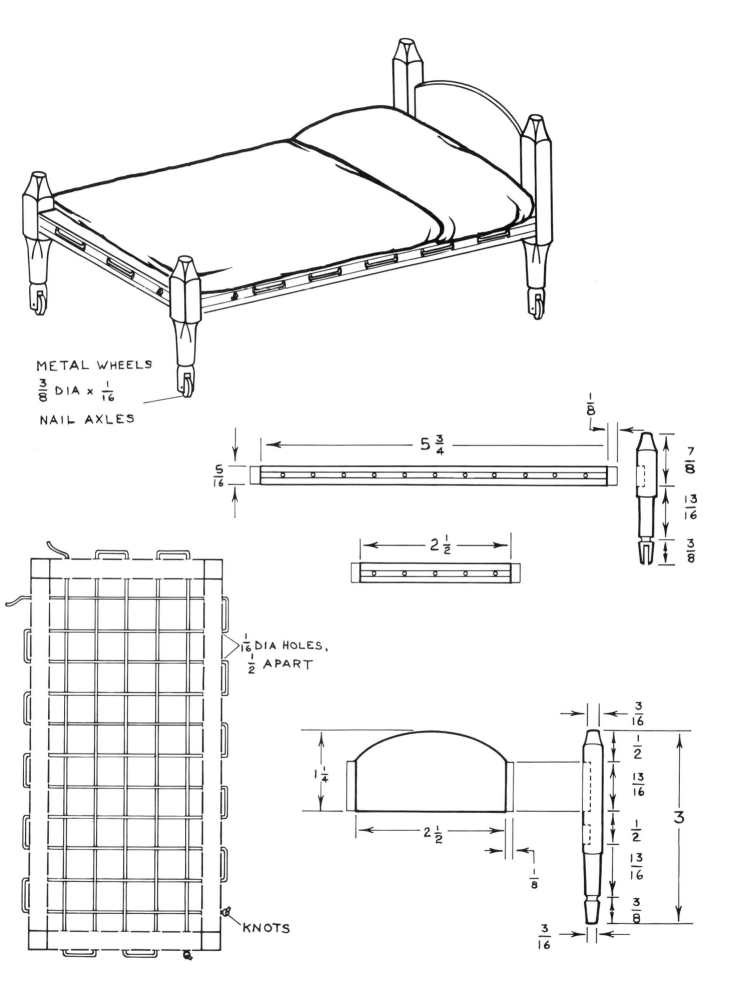

METAL WHEELS
$\frac{3}{8}$ DIA x $\frac{1}{16}$

NAIL AXLES

$\frac{1}{8}$

$5\frac{3}{4}$

$\frac{5}{16}$

$2\frac{1}{2}$

$\frac{7}{8}$

$\frac{13}{16}$

$\frac{3}{8}$

$\frac{1}{16}$ DIA HOLES,
$\frac{1}{2}$ APART

KNOTS

$\frac{3}{16}$

$\frac{1}{2}$

$\frac{13}{16}$

$\frac{1}{2}$

$\frac{13}{16}$

$\frac{3}{8}$

3

$1\frac{1}{4}$

$2\frac{1}{2}$

$\frac{1}{8}$

$\frac{3}{16}$

Utility Table

As was noted earlier, there were many variations in style and design of Shaker tables. They came in all sizes ranging from the beautiful candlestand to the long trestle dining table. This utility table is one of many that had no specific purpose but yet could be used for any number of things. Today we would call it a good "all-round" table.

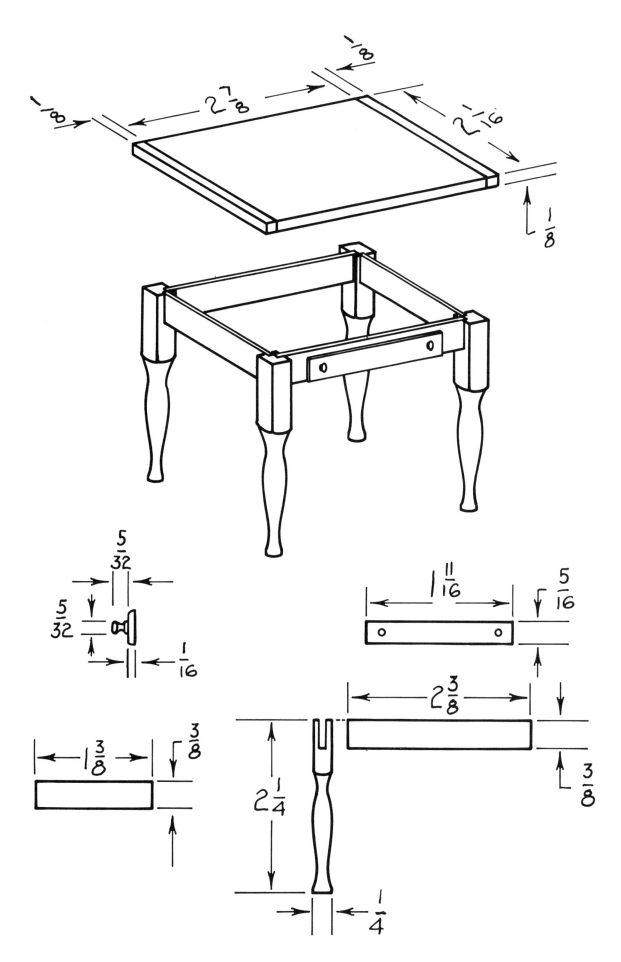

Cupboard

In the Shaker village, there was always great need for a lot of storage area for all types of articles, including clothing, sheets, and towels. The Shakers were particularly inventive when it came to chests and great numbers of doors and drawers. They perfected the style of built-in furniture and produced many pieces of furniture in which enormous amounts of articles could be neatly stored. The cupboard-chest combined both drawers and shelves in a distinctive manner, and when set against the simple, unadorned white walls, they assumed a very special interior dignity.

Since neatness and order were important precepts in their lifestyle, the Shakers excelled at placing their private goods in an orderly and efficient manner.

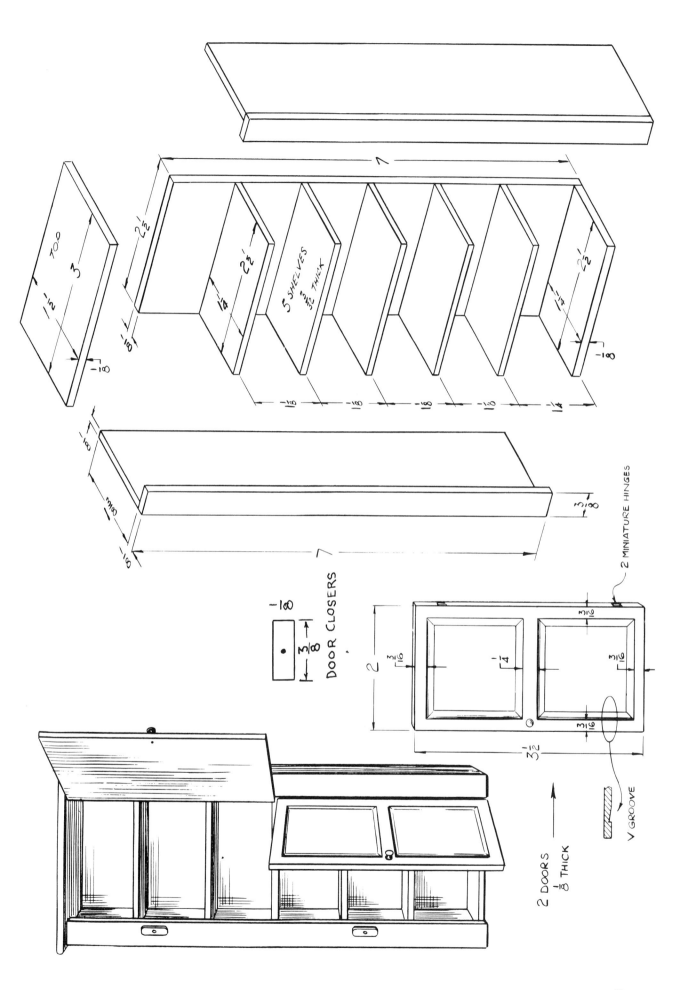

TOP

$\frac{1}{12}$

3

$\frac{1}{8}$

$2\frac{1}{2}$

1

$\frac{1}{16}$

$2\frac{1}{2}$

$1\frac{1}{4}$

5 SHELVES $\frac{3}{32}$ THICK

$2\frac{1}{2}$

$1\frac{1}{4}$

$\frac{1}{8}$

$\frac{1}{16}$ $\frac{1}{16}$ $\frac{1}{16}$ $\frac{1}{16}$ $1\frac{1}{4}$

$\frac{1}{8}$

$\frac{9}{16}$

$\frac{3}{16}$

$\frac{1}{8}$

7

2 MINIATURE HINGES

$\frac{3}{16}$

DOOR CLOSERS

$\frac{1}{8}$

$\frac{5}{8}$

2

$\frac{3}{16}$

$1\frac{1}{4}$

$\frac{3}{16}$

$\frac{3}{16}$

$3\frac{1}{2}$

V GROOVE

2 DOORS $\frac{1}{8}$ THICK

61

Blanket Chest

The blanket chest was a typical item in Colonial New England and often contained one or two drawers for storage. Thus, the Shakers improved on a form in such a way that it does have a distinctive quality. The Shaker blanket chest was always well-made and displayed fine dovetailing. Often it was stained or painted red.

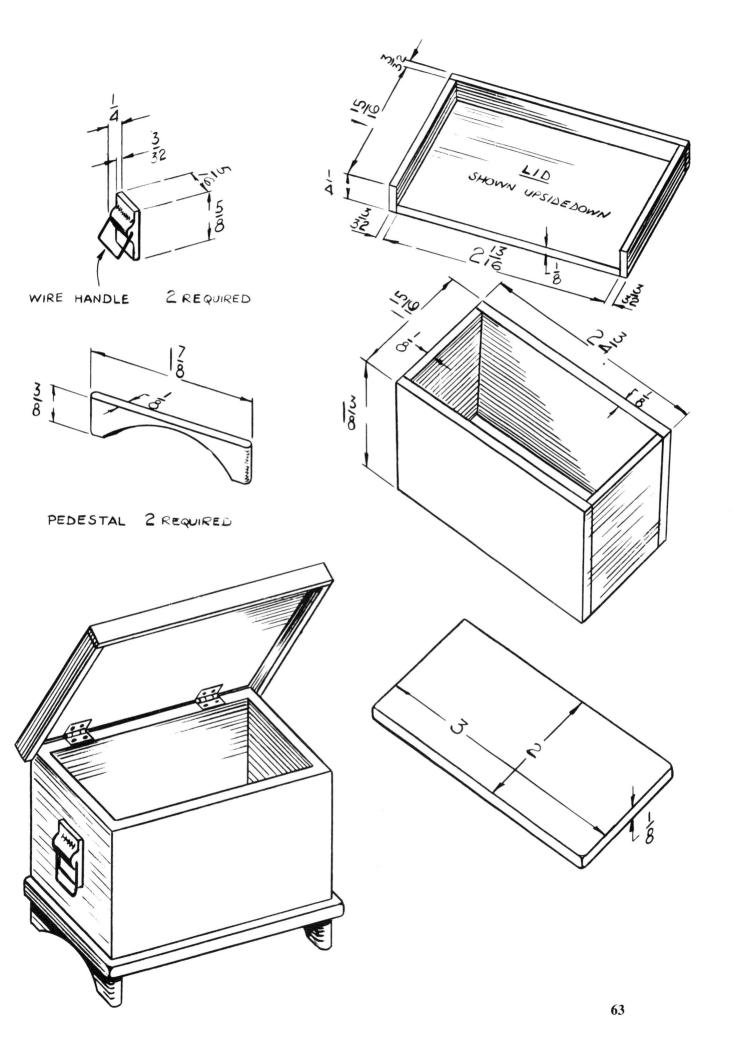

$\frac{1}{4}$

$\frac{3}{32}$

$1 \frac{5}{16}$

$\frac{5}{8}$

WIRE HANDLE   2 REQUIRED

$1 \frac{7}{8}$

$\frac{3}{8}$

$1 \frac{3}{8}$

PEDESTAL   2 REQUIRED

$3 \frac{3}{32}$

$1 \frac{5}{16}$

$\frac{1}{4}$

$3 \frac{3}{32}$

$2 \frac{13}{16}$

$\frac{1}{8}$

$3 \frac{3}{32}$

LID
SHOWN UPSIDEDOWN

$1 \frac{5}{16}$

$1 \frac{3}{8}$

$1 \frac{3}{8}$

$1 \frac{3}{8}$

$2 \frac{3}{4}$

$1 \frac{1}{8}$

$1 \frac{1}{8}$

3

2

$\frac{1}{8}$

Dry Sink

Today it is difficult for us to imagine a time when there existed no hot and cold running water. However, the time did exist when water had to be carried from a well and placed in a pitcher or receptacle before a person could wash. This solid and durable form is typical of a Shaker dry sink. It combined a drawer and shelves in such a way that a fine piece of furniture resulted.

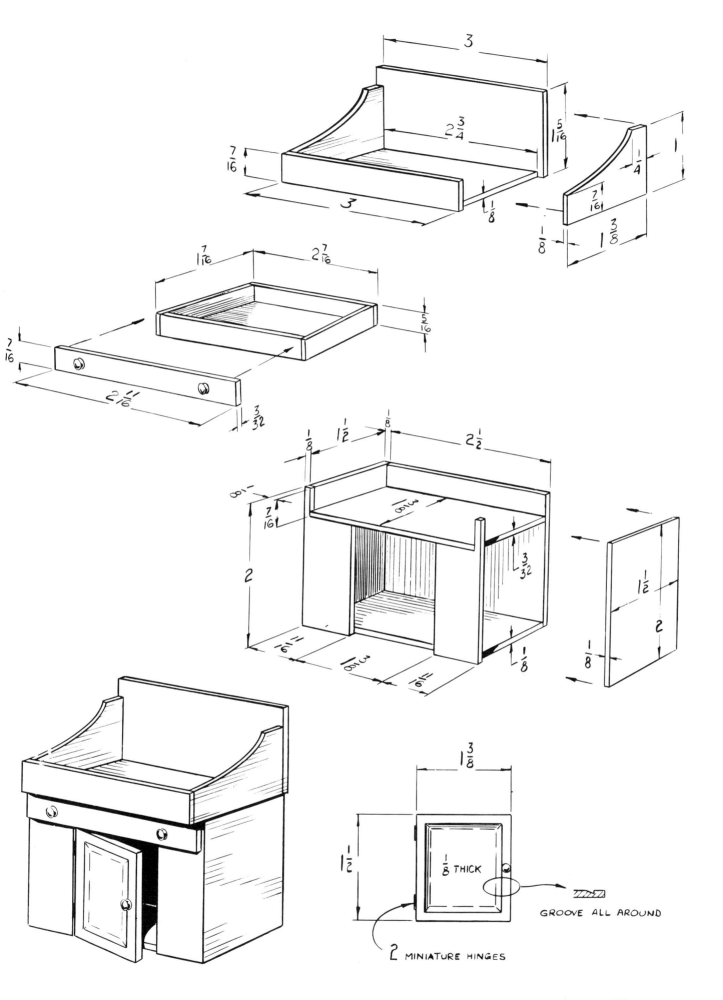

3

$2\frac{3}{4}$

$\frac{5}{16}$

1

$\frac{7}{16}$

3

$\frac{1}{8}$

$\frac{1}{4}$

$\frac{7}{16}$

$\frac{1}{8}$

$1\frac{3}{8}$

$1\frac{7}{16}$

$2\frac{7}{16}$

$\frac{15}{16}$

$\frac{7}{16}$

$2\frac{11}{16}$

$\frac{3}{32}$

$\frac{1}{8}$

$1\frac{1}{2}$

$\frac{1}{8}$

$2\frac{1}{2}$

$\frac{1}{8}$

$\frac{7}{16}$

$\frac{3}{8}$

$\frac{3}{32}$

2

$1\frac{11}{16}$

$1\frac{3}{16}$

$1\frac{1}{16}$

$\frac{1}{8}$

$1\frac{1}{2}$

2

$\frac{1}{8}$

$1\frac{3}{8}$

$1\frac{1}{2}$

$\frac{1}{8}$ THICK

GROOVE ALL AROUND

2 MINIATURE HINGES

65

Candle Sconces

Since candles were for a long time the main lighting device, the candle sconce was an important feature of a Shaker room. Candle-making was an early successful occupation of the Shaker sisters, who produced candles for the communities' needs as well as for sale to the outside world.

The unique characteristic of the Shaker candle sconce is that it had a hole from which it could be suspended from the pegboard. Kentucky sconces were know for a series of holes, one above the other, so that the sconce could be hung on pegs at graduated heights, thus, making it an adjustable holder.

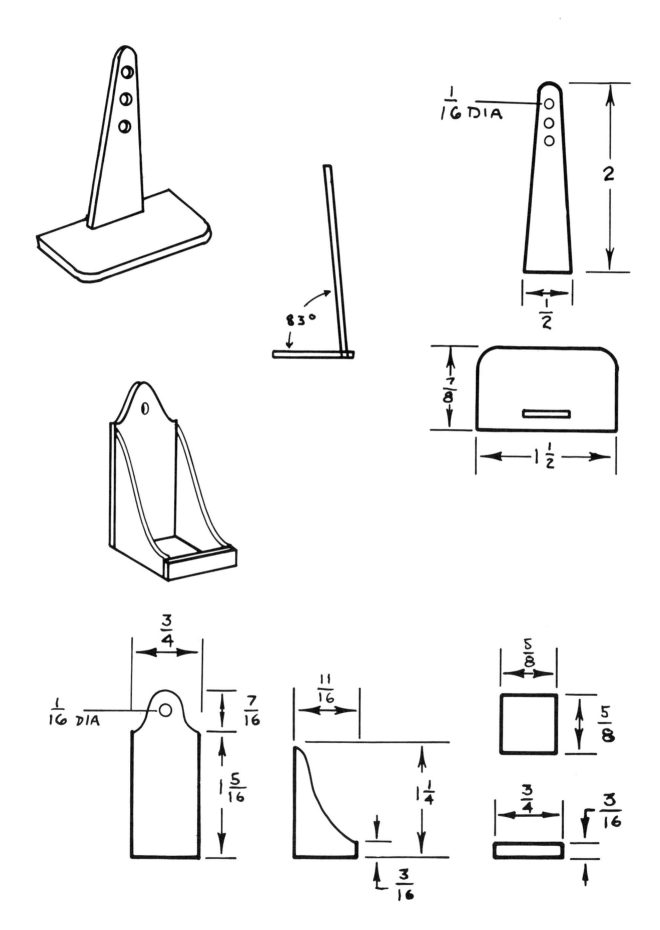

$\frac{1}{16}$ DIA

2

$\frac{1}{2}$

$\frac{7}{8}$

$1\frac{1}{2}$

83°

$\frac{3}{4}$

$\frac{1}{16}$ DIA

$\frac{7}{16}$

$1\frac{5}{16}$

$\frac{11}{16}$

$1\frac{1}{4}$

$\frac{3}{16}$

$\frac{5}{8}$

$\frac{5}{8}$

$\frac{3}{4}$

$\frac{3}{16}$

Oval Boxes and Spit Box

Wood oval boxes had been made in New England for many years, but it was the Shakers that gave the form a refined image. Their simple grace was symbolic of the Shakers' striving for perfection.

The basic innovation was the use of "fingers" or "lappers" in the joinery. A wide thin piece of maple was cut at one end with a template into "fingers." The piece was then steamed and wrapped around an oval mold with the "fingers" secured by tiny copper nails. Discs of pine were then fitted into the base and cover.

These boxes were manufactured from about 1798 to about 1960 at Sabbathday Lake, Maine. Although there are many reproductions today, no one has been able to reproduce the exact proportions, fit, and finish that made the Shaker oval box unique.

The spit box, usually painted yellow or orange, was made in the same manner as the oval box. These were common in the early 1800s, filled with sawdust or wood shavings, and used in the brothers' bedrooms or shops.

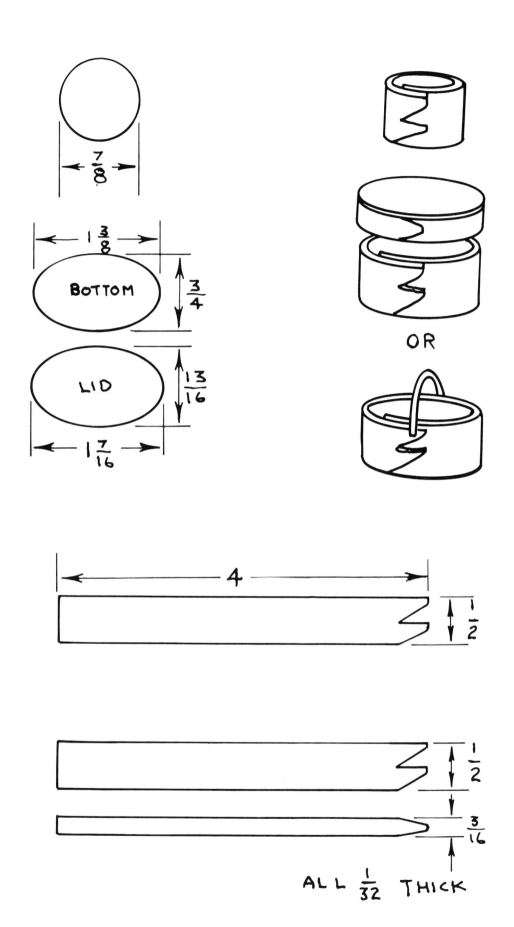

$\frac{7}{8}$

$1\frac{3}{8}$

BOTTOM

$\frac{3}{4}$

LID

$\frac{13}{16}$

$1\frac{7}{16}$

OR

4

$\frac{1}{2}$

$\frac{1}{2}$

$\frac{3}{16}$

ALL $\frac{1}{32}$ THICK

Bonnet Mold

The woven straw or palm-leaf bonnet was an important part of the Shaker sisters' ''going out'' dress. It was also a product sold to the outside world during the mid-1800s. These bonnets were trimmed with a short silk cape at the back of the neck and with ribbons for fastening under the chin.

To fashion a bonnet after the palm leaf had been sized and dampened, the pieces were split and on hand looms, woven with thread. The pieces were then shaped or molded on a mold of the type pictured. The head form could be placed at a convenient working height by inserting the rod in a hole bored at the top of the upright piece or in holes bored slantwise near the top.

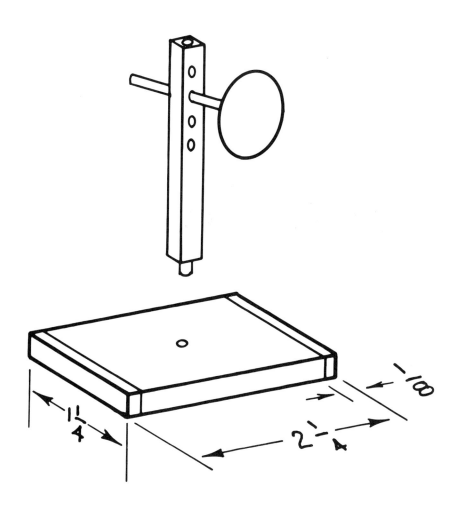

$1\frac{1}{4}$

$2\frac{1}{4}$

$\frac{1}{8}$

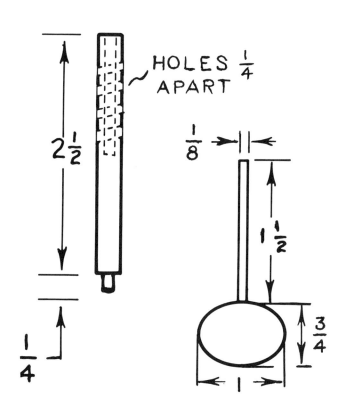

HOLES $\frac{1}{4}$ APART

$2\frac{1}{2}$

$\frac{1}{4}$

$\frac{1}{8}$

$1\frac{1}{2}$

$\frac{3}{4}$

Hanging Towel Rack

Even the smallest items exhibit characteristics of a certain style. This is evident in the hanging towel rack. The same faithful attention to detail that has been seen in chairs and cupboards is also seen in the simple utilitarian design of this everyday article. It has an upper rail by which it can be hung from the Shaker pegboard.

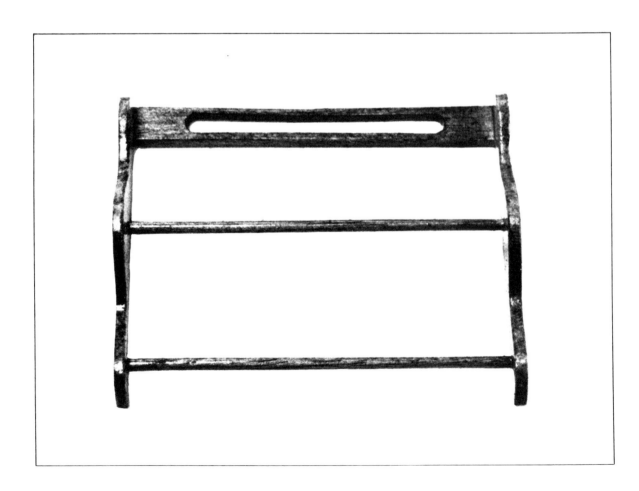

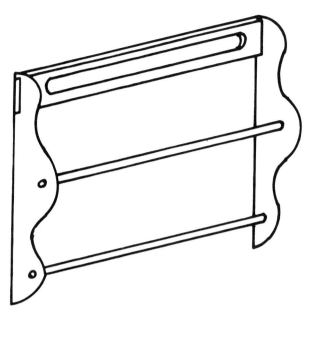

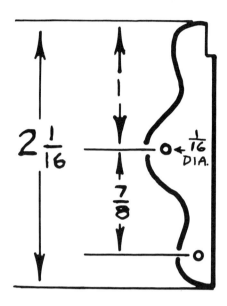

$2\frac{1}{16}$

$\frac{7}{8}$

$\leftarrow\frac{1}{16}$ DIA.

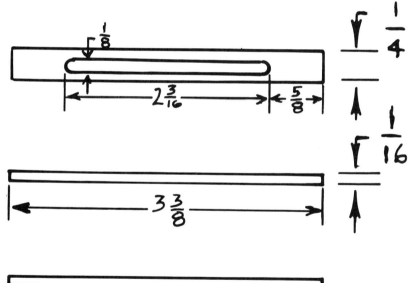

$\frac{1}{8}$

$2\frac{3}{16}$

$\frac{5}{8}$

$\frac{1}{4}$

$\frac{1}{16}$

$3\frac{3}{8}$

Floor Towel Rack

Order necessitated the construction of a great number of chests, cases of drawers, closets, and racks since all clothing, utensils, and textiles had to be put away or in its proper place. Here the simple use of three horizontal pieces of wood balanced exactly on two rounded supports give the towel rack a forthright and sturdy form.

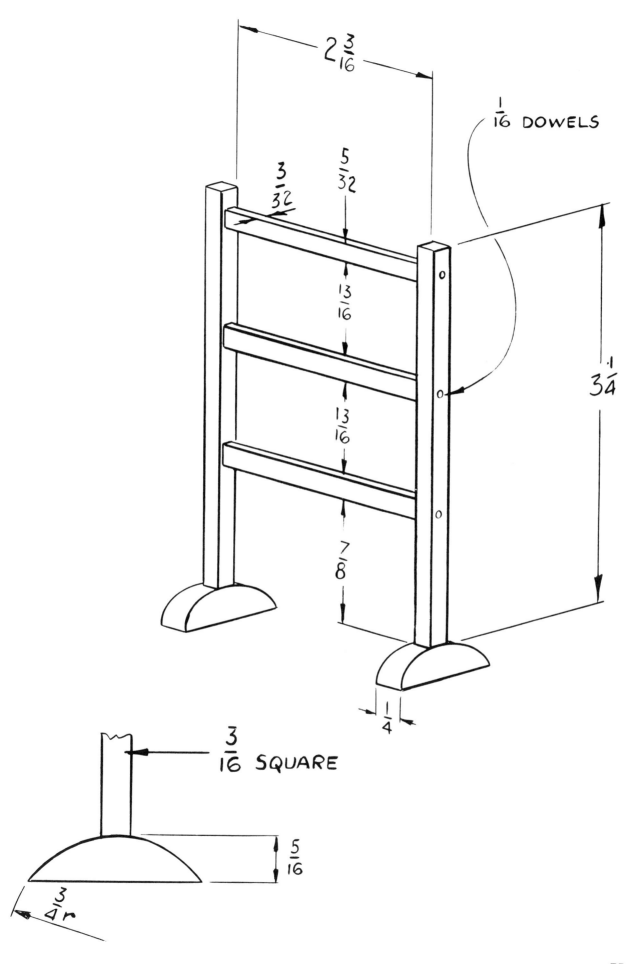

$2\frac{3}{16}$

$\frac{1}{16}$ DOWELS

$\frac{3}{32}$

$\frac{5}{32}$

$\frac{13}{16}$

$\frac{13}{16}$

$3\frac{1}{4}$

$\frac{7}{8}$

$\frac{1}{4}$

$\frac{3}{16}$ SQUARE

$\frac{5}{16}$

$\frac{3}{4}r$

75

Step Stools

The next three articles comprise the one-step, two-step, and three-step stools. Each had the same function. Usually constructed out of pine, these were used so that a person could reach the top drawers or compartments of a high Shaker cupboard or built-in unit. Since the average person in the last century was much shorter than his counterpart today, we can readily understand the need for these stools, commonly referred to as "steppers."

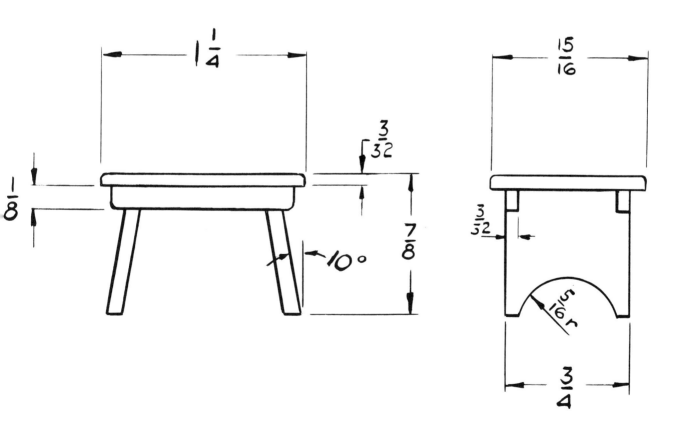

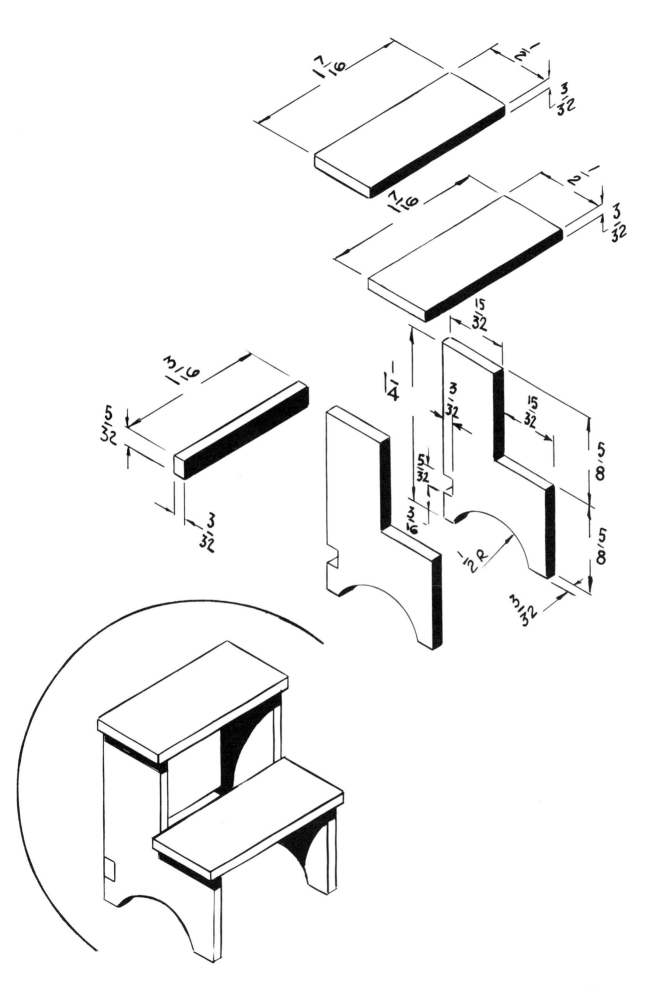

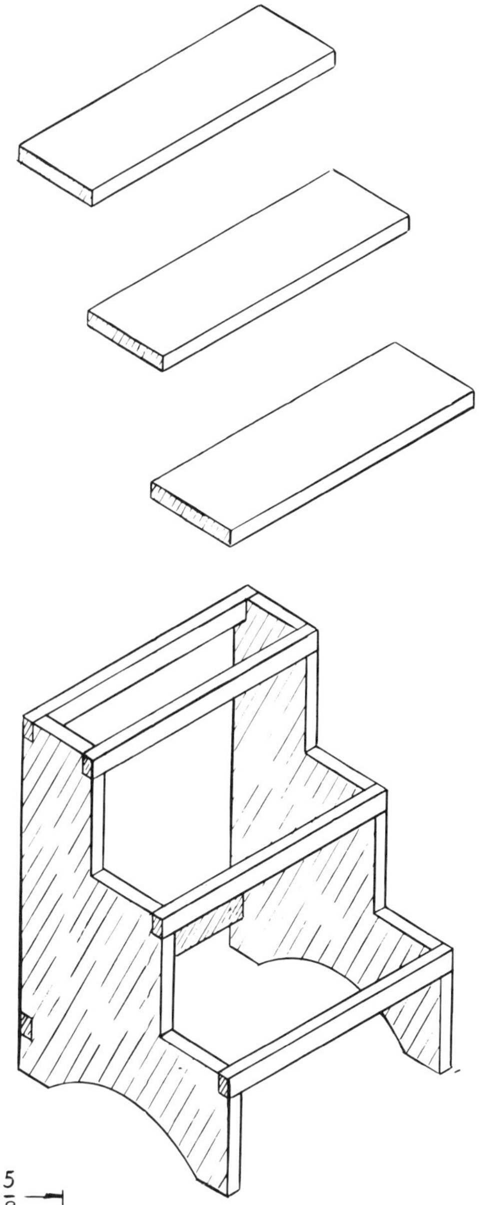

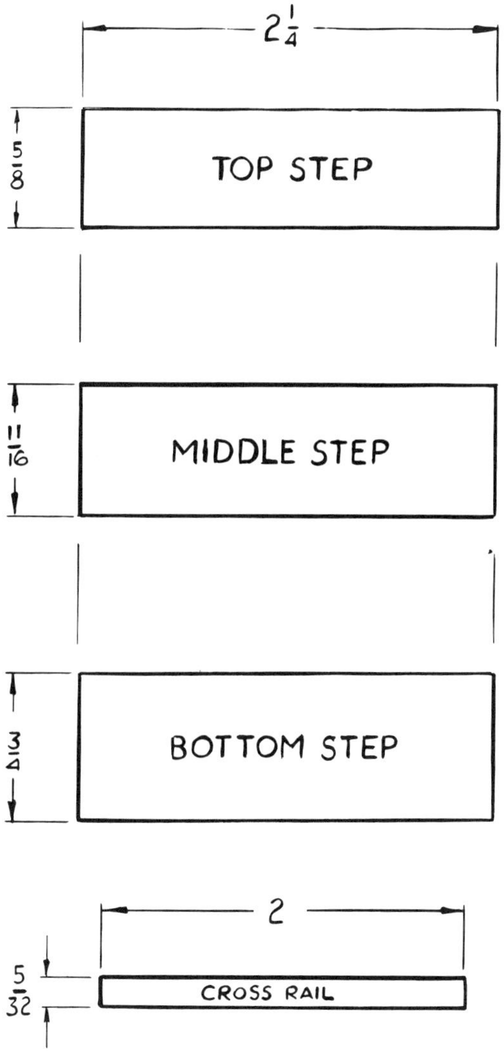

2 1/4
5/8
TOP STEP
11/16
MIDDLE STEP
3/4
BOTTOM STEP
2
5/32
CROSS RAIL

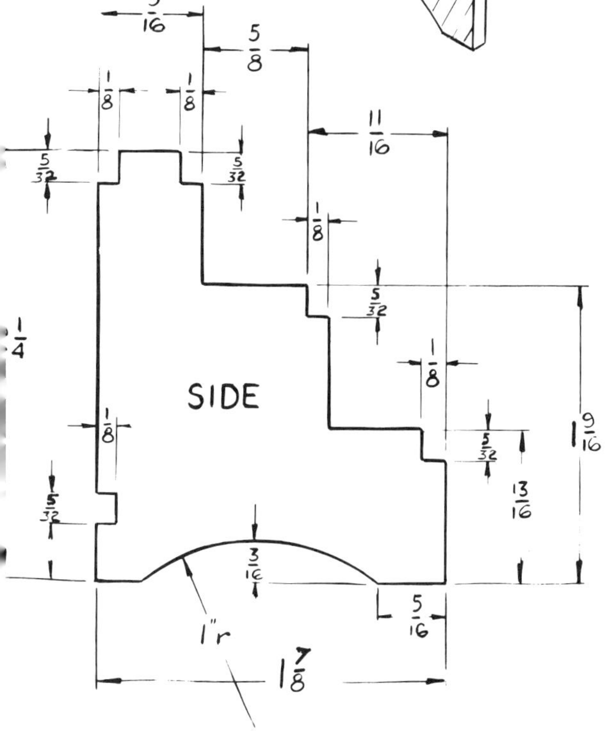

9/16
5/8
1/8
1/8
5/32
5/32
11/16
1/8
5/32
1/4
1/8
SIDE
1/8
5/32
1 9/16
13/16
5/32
3/16
5/16
1"r
1 7/8

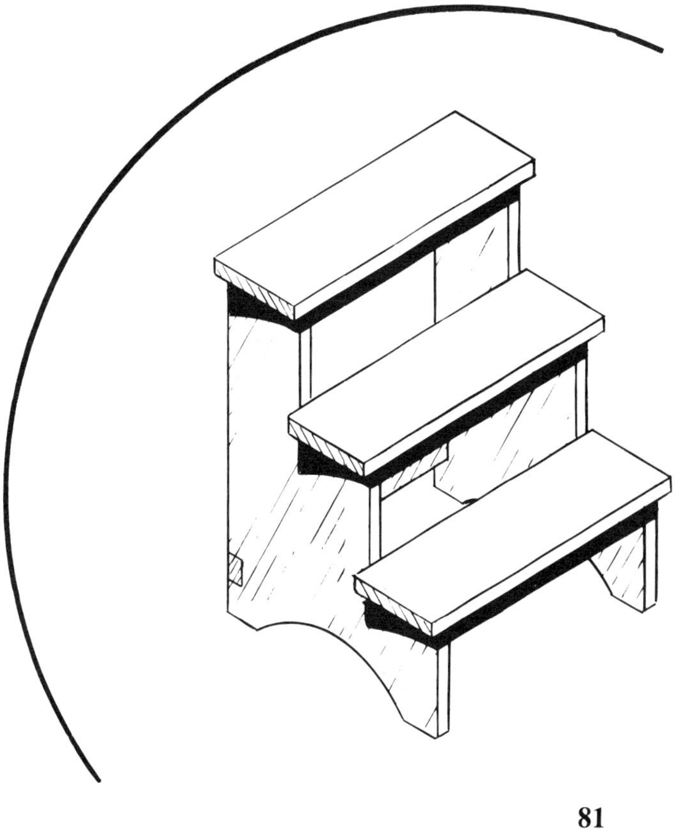

Wood Carrier   Dough Box

Boxes with handles were called carriers. This particular wood carrier or "chip-box," rectangular in shape but still graceful in proportion, was used in many communities to hold kindling, dry sticks, or chips of wood, which had to be gathered at the woodhouse.

The doughbox was a kitchen necessity at a time when convenience foods and processors did not exist. Bread dough, enough to take care of the needs of the whole community, would be kept in this wood box so that it could rise in the kitchen's warm air.

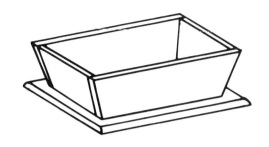

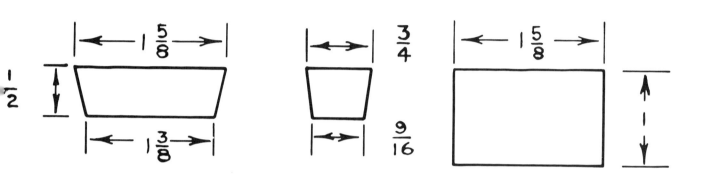

$1\frac{5}{8}$

$1\frac{3}{8}$

$1\frac{1}{2}$

$\frac{3}{4}$

$\frac{9}{16}$

$1\frac{5}{8}$

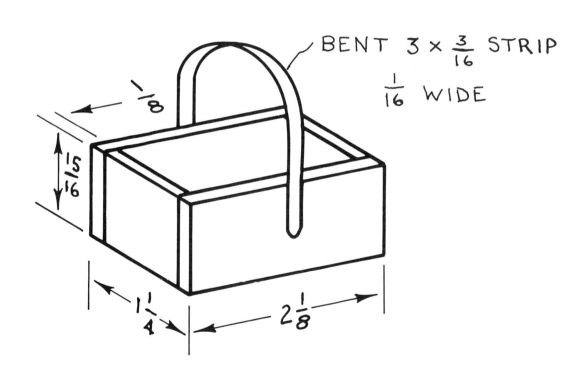

BENT $3 \times \frac{3}{16}$ STRIP

$\frac{1}{16}$ WIDE

$1\frac{1}{8}$

$\frac{15}{16}$

$1\frac{1}{4}$

$2\frac{1}{8}$

Shoemaker's Candlestand

As in all the various industrial shops of the Shakers, it was often necessary to work indoors by candlelight. This adjustable candlestand, used in the shoemaker's shop, is a reminder to us of the diligence of Shaker labor. It consists of a stem which is threaded and set into a base. The double arm holds two candles at a given height. The tin, iron, or steel candlesticks used on stands such as these would also have been manufactured in the Shakers' own workshops.

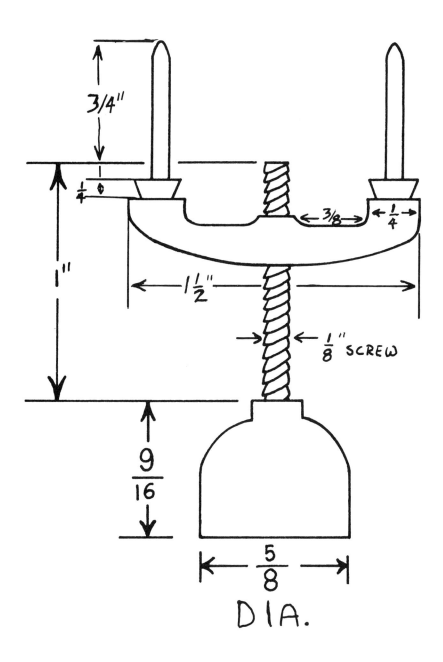

3/4"

1/4

3/8

1/4

1"

1½"

1/8" SCREW

9/16

5/8

DIA.

Pegboard

It is not surprising that throughout the different communities similar forms and designs appear and reappear. Every community was modeled after that of Mt. Lebanon and followed the Millenial Laws, the central body of Shaker laws that covered all aspects of Shaker life. The Central Ministry in Mt. Lebanon exerted a certain amount of control through its own supervision, exchange visits, and correspondence. Although there were some regional differences, for the most part, all Shaker communities were united on such topics as the furnishing of rooms and the basic design of most pieces of furniture. There was not an exact uniformity but certainly a very great similarity.

Through every community, against the white walls, one would see the ever-present and ever-useful Shaker pegboard with rows upon rows of wooden pegs. This more than anything else was the true symbol of Shaker order. Anything could hang from the pegs—dresses, coats, bonnets, household utensils, chairs, tools, brushes, clocks, etc.

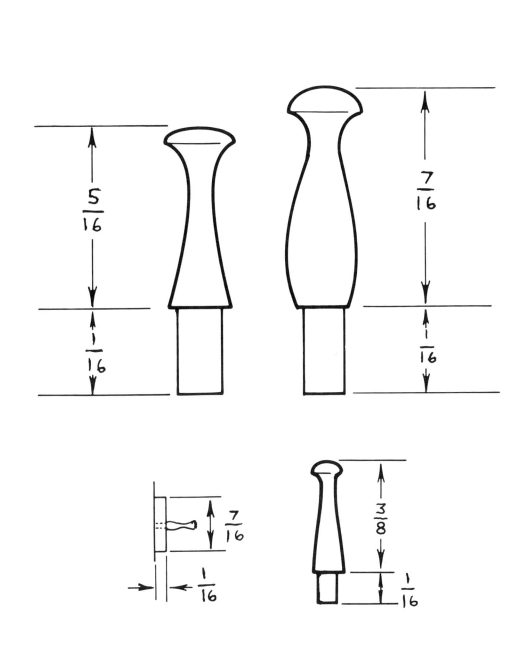

Wood Box

Large wooden boxes with side pegs for holding dustpan and brush were used in halls, some bedrooms, and shops to hold fuel for small wood-burning stoves.

The concept of one piece of furniture having a dual purpose was one the Shaker liked.

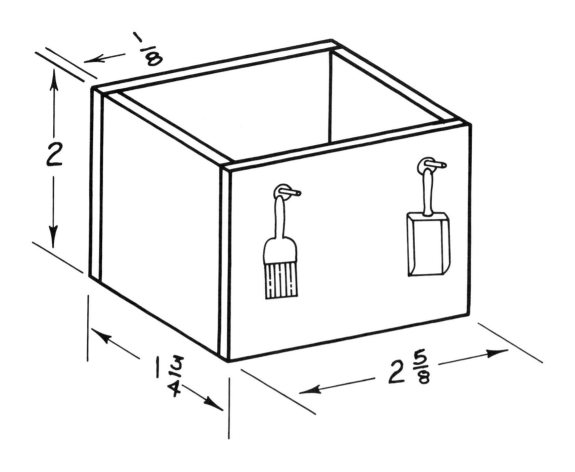

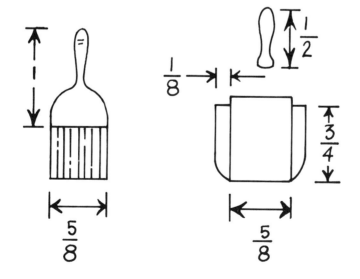

Hanging Mirror

In the early Shaker years, the use of the mirror was a controversial subject. On one hand, it was considered a luxury and an instrument of vanity; on the other hand, it helped promote order and personal grooming. In the Millenial Laws of 1845, we read the following concerning its use in the bedroom, "A little glass, perhaps eight or ten inches square may be placed in every room, but no particular one ought to own a looking glass of any size whatever."

It was customarily outfitted with frames or moldings mitered at the corners. These frames, fitted with a mirror, were then fitted into a grooved base of a rack, similar to a T-square, which was perforated at the top so that it could be hung on a pegboard.

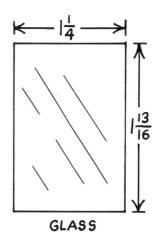

GLASS

$1\frac{1}{4}$

$1\frac{13}{16}$

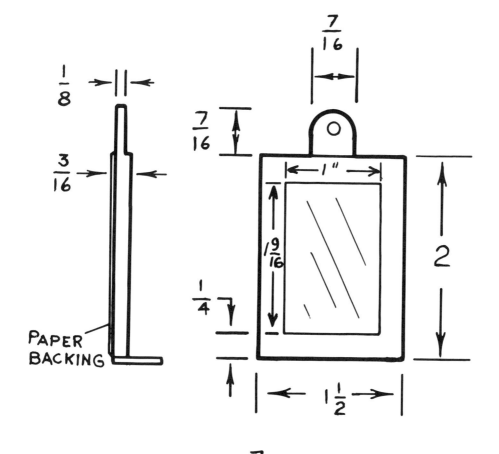

$\frac{1}{8}$

$\frac{3}{16}$

PAPER
BACKING

$\frac{7}{16}$

$\frac{7}{16}$

$1''$

$1\frac{9}{16}$

$\frac{1}{4}$

2

$1\frac{1}{2}$

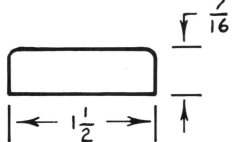

$\frac{7}{16}$

$1\frac{1}{2}$

Instructions for Weaving Chair Seats

Iron-on rug binding closely resembles the "listing" of the Shakers and can be easily woven into a chair seat. If the iron-on variety is not available, use regular rug binding and back it with Mystic tape so that it will be stiff and hold its shape. It must then be cut into 1/16-inch-wide pieces. A solid color may be used or two different colors can be alternated to give a more noticeable checkerboard pattern.

The first step in seating the chair is known as *warping*. This simply entails wrapping the binding around the front and back seat rails to provide a warp both on the top and the bottom of the seat. The procedure is as follows: the end (doubled over for strength) of one piece or coil of binding is glued with contact cement to the inner side of the back rail as close as possible to the left back post; this doubled-over end must point toward the top of the chair. The binding is brought over the back rail to the front rail at right angles to both the front and back rails. It is then brought over the front rail and returned to the back rail, which it goes under and over. DO NOT TWIST THE BINDING. Continue until the back right post is reached. Then bring the binding over and under the front rail and back to the back rail and cut off the excess, allowing about ¼-inch extra length. This end is doubled over and securely tucked in. Do not allow the binding to sag; take out as much of the slack as possible so the seat will be firm.

When the warp is completed, the next step is the actual weaving of the seat. This is begun by securing the end of the piece or coil of binding, which will be the *weft*. The end, doubled over for strength, is glued to the inside of the left side rail as close as possible to the left back post. The free end is then attached to a large needle with thread and brought over the first warp strip of the top layer, under the next, over one, under one, etc. until the right back post is reached. The full length of the binding is pulled through all the top layers of warp strips. The chair is turned over and the process is repeated on the lower layer of warp strips.

Next, the weft is again woven through the top layer of warp strips, starting under the first strip, over the second, etc. so that the result is the start of a checkerboard pattern. The chair is again turned over and the weft is returned through the lower level of warp strips so as to form, as on the top layer, the beginning of a checkerboard pattern. The process described above is continued until the weft reaches the front posts of the chair. Again, it must be emphasized that the binding must not be twisted. Also, it should be pulled firmly each time it is brought through the warp strips, and the rows should be kept as straight as possible, each touching the last. All ends should be tucked securely into place, and the seat will be finished.

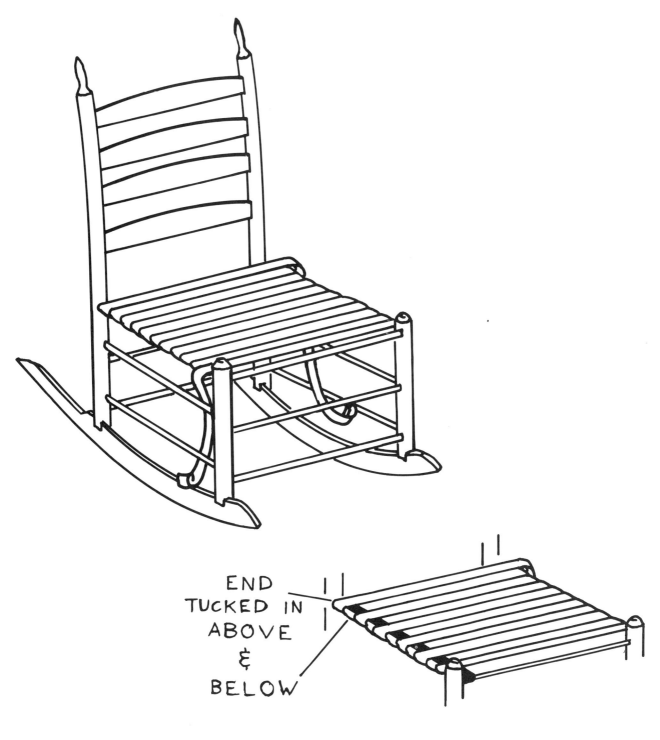

END
TUCKED IN
ABOVE
&
BELOW

WEAVE
ON RAIL

END
TUCKED IN

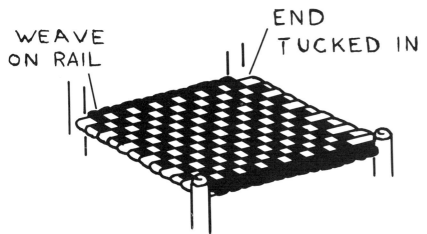

Instructions for Constructing a Shaker Room

For the floor, use ¾-inch clear pine or maple. For the walls, use ¼-inch Baltic birch plywood. If this is not available, use a fine plywood with two good sides.

Cut the floor and walls to measurements as directed on the measured drawing. Stain the floor with Minwax stain of Colonial Maple. Score with a dull pencil to look like the planks of a wooden floor. Paint the walls with two coats of white undercoating and two coats of flat white paint.

Assemble the walls and floor together. Cut the window to size, and stain and lay it in. A commercial pre-assembled kit of the proper size may be used. Place the window stays inside and outside.

Place hinged molding on the door. Cut, score, and stain the door. Then hang it in the wall. Complete the door moldings. Lay in the baseboard. Assemble and stain the pegboards and mount them in room. Now you are ready to furnish the room.

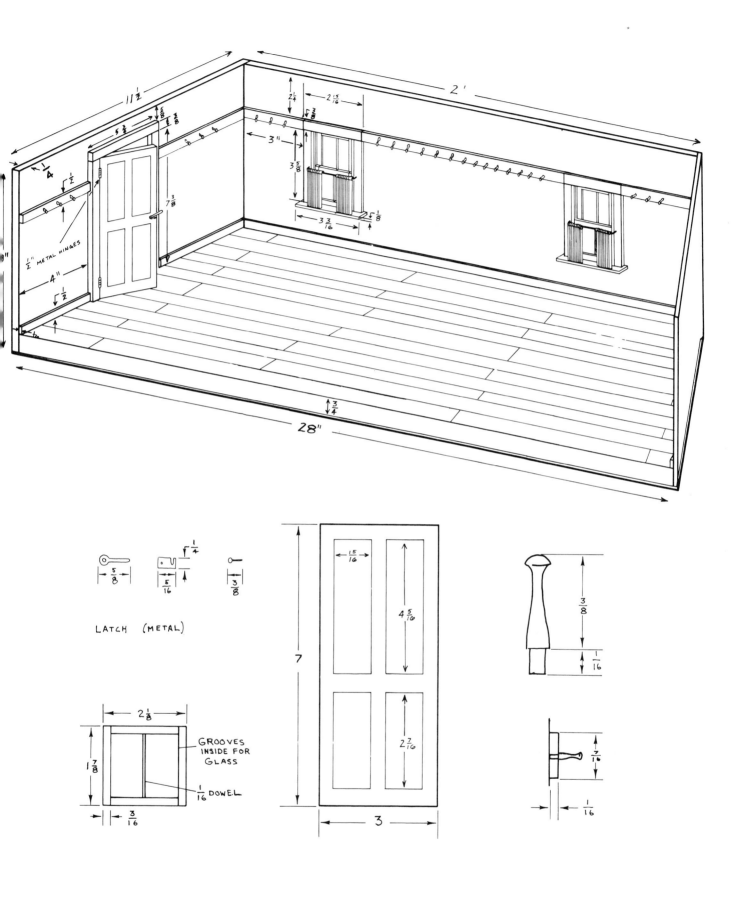

LATCH (METAL)

GROOVES
INSIDE FOR
GLASS

$\frac{1}{16}$ DOWEL

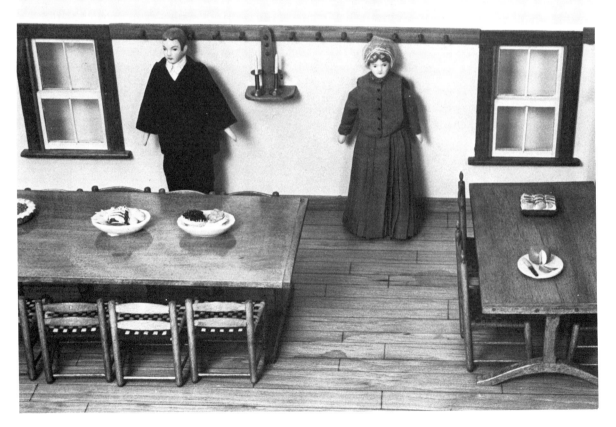

Suppliers

Wood

The miniaturist's greatest joy is the knowledge that he has made something with his own hands. It is not easy to handcraft a fine miniature; but with hard work and practice, you can gradually gain an expertise that you hardly felt was possible. How rewarding it is!

The high quality of Shaker miniatures emanates from each simple line. One reason why they look so fine is that native American woods have been used to make them. Long ago, the Shaker craftsman used only woods he could find around the Shaker village. Exotic woods, such as mahogany and rosewood, were not used. The woods most used in fine cabinet work were pine, maple, cherry, and butternut. The graining of the woods today is much admired for its own natural beauty.

Fine quality native woods on a limited scale are slowly becoming available for the miniature woodworker throughout the many miniature shops and craft stores. Most miniature lumber is made from basswood, a soft wood like pine but with little graining. This is not the best material for carrying out the measured drawings in this book. Basswood does not give the high caliber appearance that is so essential to Shaker miniatures.

To build the furniture from scratch, you can buy boards of fine pine or maple and cut them to the required thickness. You may also be able to find miniature lumber in the small sizes that you will need. There are a number of miniature shops and outlets where native American woods can be purchased. Below is a listing of some firms that feature such woods:

Architectural Model Supplies, Inc.
115-B Bellam Boulevard
P. O. Box 3497
San Rafael, CA 94902
All building supplies, tools, and adhesives.
    Send $2.50 for illustrated catalog.

Carlson's Miniatures
899 Industrial Drive
West Chicago, IL 60185
Tel. (312) 231-7046
Dollhouse components, including windows,
    bricks, and pine boards for flooring, paneling,
    and furniture making.

The Dollhouse Factory
P.O. Box 456
157 Main Street
Lebanon, NJ 08833
Tel. (201) 236-6404
All kinds of dollhouse supplies and tools.
    Limited amount of hardwoods. Catalog costs
    $1.00.

The Enchanted Doll House
Manchester Center, VT 05255
Tel. (802) 362-1327
A complete doll and miniature catalog is
    available for $2.00 mailing list fee.
    Hardwoods are available on a limited basis.

H. L. Childs & Son
25 State Street
P.O. Box 355
Northampton, MA 01060
Miniature lumber supplies and building
material. Custom made doors and windows.
Catalog costs $1.00.

Miniatures By Allen
RR 2, P.O. Box 183
Sherman, CT 06784
Tel. (203) 354-0771
Oak, pine, walnut, birch, and mahogany for
paneling, flooring, clapboard siding, and
miniature furniture. Also, wood strip
shingles. Send self-addressed, stamped
envelope for price list.

Shaker Miniatures
2913 Hunting Road
Cleveland, OH 44120
Tel. (216) 751-5963
Cedar, ash, cherry in four widths as well as
walnut, butternut, oak, quarter oak, poplar,
maple and turning squares. Send
self-addressed, stamped (2 stamps) envelope
for catalog.

Northeastern Scale Models, Inc.
P.O. Box 425
Methuen, MA 01844
Limited amount of walnut available. Send
self-addressed, stamped envelope for price
list.

Tools

Brookstone Company
Brookstone Building
126 Vose Farm Road
Peterborough, NH 03458

X-Acto (the largest manufacturer of miniature
tools)
45-35 Van Dam Street
Long Island City, NY 11101
Order direct from X-Acto or ask them to send
you the names of stores in your area who
carry their tools.

Woodcraft Supply Corp.
313 Montvale Avenue
Woburn, MA 01801

Dremel Manufacturing Division (power tools)
Emerson Electric Company
4915 21st Street
Racine, WI 53406
Order direct from Dremel by mail or ask them
to send you the names of stores in your area
who carry their tools.

Hinges

The Brickyard
Newcastle, ME 04553
Full line of miniature brass hinges, including H,
HL, T, and butt with pins. Send
self-addressed, stamped envelope for
information.

Philip J. Grande
513 East Orange Grove Avenue
Burbank, CA 91501
Send $1.25 for color catalog of brass
mini-hinges.

Shaker cast-metal stoves

Shaker Stoves
P.O. Box 207
Charlestown, MA 02129
Send self-addressed, stamped envelope for
brochure.

Shaker-inspired paint and finishes

Guild of Shaker Crafts
401 West Savidge Street
Spring Lake, MI 49456
Samples available on request. Catalog costs
$2.50.

Shaker Museums and Collections

The following is a list of permanent collections of Shaker furniture and articles. Hours and fees are not given because they are subject to change. Please contact the museum directly for more specific information.

An asterisk * beside the museum name means that Shaker miniature furniture and accessories are sold in the gift shop.

Delaware

The Henry Francis DuPont Winterthur
  Museum
Winterthur, DE 19735
Tel. (302) 656-8591
Open year round
Two recreated Shaker rooms may be seen on
  the Museum tours. Reservations are
  required.

District of Columbia

Smithsonian Institution
  Museum of History and Technology
  Hall of Everyday Life in the American Past
Washington, D.C. 20560
Tel. (202) 381-5415
Open year round
A platform exhibition of Shaker furniture and
  artifacts.

Kentucky

Western Kentucky University
  Kentucky Museum
Kentucky Building
Bowling Green, KY 42101
Tel. (502) 745-2592
Open year round, Tuesday–Saturday 11–4.
  Closed Sundays and Mondays.
The life and history of Kentucky's people as
interpreted through their art, furniture, and
crafts includes a collection of furniture and
crafts from the South Union, Kentucky Shaker
Village.

*Shakertown at Pleasant Hill, Inc.
Route 4
Harrodsburg, KY 40330
Tel. (606) 734-9111
Open year round
A restored Shaker village of which
  twenty-seven original buildings remain.
  Furniture and artifacts are on display. Dining
  and overnight lodgings are available in
  original buildings. Craft demonstrations are
  given. On permanent display is an eight-room
  miniature Shaker brick building furnished
  with Shaker miniatures.

*Shakertown at South Union
South Union, KY 42283
Tel. (502) 542-4167
Open May–October
A large collection of furniture, crafts, and
    artifacts dating back to South Union's early
    days are displayed in two original Shaker
    buildings. The annual Shaker Festival held in
    July features Shaker songs and dances during
    a drama telling the history of the South
    Union colony from 1807–1922.

Maine

*United Society of Shakers
Sabbathday Lake
Poland Spring, ME 04274
Tel. (207) 926-4391
Open May–September. Closed Sundays
An original Shaker village founded in 1793 and
    still occupied by Shaker sisters. Guide
    service. Exhibits of furniture, tin,
    woodenware, textiles, tools, and farm
    implements.

Massachusetts

Boston Museum of Fine Arts
469 Huntington Avenue
Boston, MA 02115
Tel. (617) 267-9300
Open year round. Closed Mondays.
The Eastern Shaker societies are represented in
    a recreated room with many different Shaker
    elements, including woodwork from Harvard,
    Massachusetts, furniture, stove, and
    miscellaneous artifacts.

Fruitlands Museum
Prospect Hill
Harvard, MA 04151
Tel. (617) 456-3924
Open May–September
The Museum includes Fruitlands, the early
    eighteenth century farmhouse where Bronson
    Alcott and leaders of the Transcendental
    Movement attempted a new social order and
    a Shaker house, moved from the Harvard,
    Massachusetts community furnished with
    furniture, artifacts, and textiles.

*Hancock Shaker Village
U.S. Route 20
Hancock, MA 01237
Mailing Address: P.O. Box 898
Pittsfield, MA 01201
Tel. (413) 443-0188
Open June–October
A former Shaker community with twenty
    buildings, sixteen of which have been opened
    and outfitted with distinguished Shaker
    collections. Annual Shaker Kitchen Festival
    and "World Peoples' Dinners" are held
    periodically. Craft demonstrations.

Michigan

Henry Ford Museum
Dearborn, MI 48121
Tel. (313) 271-1620
Open year round
A small collection of Shaker furniture and
    artifacts are on display as part of the major
    collection of American Decorative Arts as
    well as other Shaker items which are on
    display in various installations.

New Hampshire

*Shaker Village, Inc.
East Canterbury, NH 03224
Tel. (603) 783-9822
Open late May–October. Closed Sundays
An original Shaker village founded in 1792.
    Starting as a one-building museum in 1959,
    each year more displays are opened to the
    public. It is still occupied by Shaker sisters.
    Guided tour is given.

New York

*Shaker Museum
Shaker Museum Road
Old Chatham, NY 12136
Tel. (518) 794-9105
Open May–October
Oldest and largest of the public museums
    devoted to Shaker crafts, including furniture,
    crafts, inventions, complete industry shops,
    and herb house. An annual flea market is
    held in August.

Ohio

Golden Lamb Hotel
Route U.S. 42
Lebanon, OH 45036
Tel. (513) 932-5065
Open year round
Oldest hostelry in Ohio, furnished with
    antiques and Shaker items. Shaker rooms are
    on display. Dining room features Shaker
    specialties. Guests stay overnight in the same
    rooms that slept Presidents McKinley,
    Adams, Grant, and Hayes.

Kettering-Moraine Museum
Kettering, OH 45439
Tel. (513) 299-2722
Open year round Sundays 1–5, during the week
    by appointment
Two Shaker rooms, one dedicated to the
    Watervliet, Ohio Shaker community and the
    other a loan exhibition of the Steven Kistler
    collection. An Ohio Shaker Festival is held in
    August.

*Shaker Historical Society
16740 South Park Boulevard
Shaker Heights, OH 44120
Tel. (216) 921-1201
Open year round in the afternoon. Closed
    Saturdays.
A large collection of Shaker furniture, crafts,
    and industries mainly from the North Union,
    Ohio Shaker community. The Museum
    property is located on land once owned by
    the North Union Shakers; the house was
    built of stone in 1910 from Shaker Mill
    Family quarry.

Warren County Historical Society
Route U.S. 42
Lebanon, OH 45036
Tel. (513) 932-1817
Open year round. Closed Mondays and
    holidays.
Shaker furniture and artifacts, many of them
    displayed in recreated Shaker rooms, are
    largely from the Union Village, Ohio Shaker
    Community, which had been located only a
    few miles away.

Western Reserve Historical Society
10825 East Boulevard
Cleveland, OH 44106
Tel. (216) 721-5722
Open year round. Closed Mondays
A fine collection of Shaker furniture, crafts,
    and artifacts as well as the largest collection
    of Shaker books and manuscripts in the
    world.

Pennsylvania

Philadelphia Museum of Art
26th Street and Benjamin Franklin Parkway
Philadelphia, PA 19130
Tel. (215) 763-8100
Open year round
A complete sisters' room from the North
    Family Dwelling in Mt. Lebanon, New York
    with built-in chests and appropriate
    furnishings. Also included is a fine collection
    of furniture and artifacts from the New
    Hampshire communities.

Vermont

Shelburne Museum
U.S. Route 7
Shelburne, VT 05482
Tel. (802) 985-3344
Open late May–October
Shaker artifacts and Shaker shed from the East
    Canterbury, New Hampshire Shaker Village.

Miniature Shows

Visiting shows is an excellent way of making new contacts, seeing new products, and communicating with people interested in the same field as you are. Ask to be on the mailing list of an organization that presents miniature craft shows. This is one way to be in periodic contact with fellow miniature enthusiasts.

The list below includes organizations and individuals that hold at least one show a year.

Lisa Bennett
P.O. Box 4061
Sarasota, FL 33571

Robert Burns
500 South Taylor Street
Arlington, VA 22204

Carriage World
Stage House Village
Scotch Plains, NJ 07076

Citizen Resource Center
Beaman Street
West Boylston, MA 01583

Cleveland Miniature Society
20391 Miller Avenue
Euclid, OH 44119

Fran and Bob Cook
P.O. Box 450
La Mirada, CA 90637

Doll Collectors of Oklahoma
c/o Mrs. Murrell Pilcher
4008 Teal Drive
Oklahoma City, OK 73115

The Emporium
P.O. Box 452
Chester, NJ 07930

H & S Miniatures
P.O. Box 419
Huntington Valley, PA 19006

Peggy Hoffman
P.O. Box 546
Cheshire, CT 06410

Ruth Kohlman
111 Sandstone Drive
Rochester, NY 14616

Jill Koons
P.O. Box 635
Bedford, PA 15522

Frances LaMonica
67 Pomona Avenue
Yonkers, NY 10703

The Little Doll House
129 Littleton Road
Westford, MA 01886

Miniature Maker's Society
c/o Jane Haskell
31 Evergreen Road
Northford, CT 06472

Miniature Showcase Productions
Motts Cove Road North
Roslyn Harbor, NY 11576

Miniature Society of Cincinnati
1021 Marion Avenue
Cincinnati, OH 45229

Kitty Osker
959 High Ridge Road
Stamford, CT 06905

William Mathers
2913 South Hayes Avenue
State Rt. 4
Sandusky, OH 44870

Pam Maxwell
310 Hillcrest Drive
Edinboro, PA 16412

Marlene Mayer
2640 Golf Road, Suite 223
Glenview, IL 60025

Miniature Enthusiasts of Toronto
171 Homewood Avenue
Willowdale, Ontario
Canada M2M 1K4

Everlyn Podesla
113 Red Bush Lane
Milford, CT 06460

San Diego Miniature Crafters
c/o Gloria Osborn
1997 Alameda Terrace
San Diego, CA 92103

Seven Limited
5316 San Pedro
San Antonio, TX 78212

Teri's Mini Workshop
Box 13028
Orlando, FL 32809

Trade Show for Miniatures
ITC
545 Fifth Avenue
New York, NY 10017

Wee Bees Show
c/o Miniature Makers Workshop
677 South Eaton
Birmingham, MI 48012

Yankee Miniatures
20 Sunset Hill Avenue
Norwalk, CT 06851

Miniature Publications

The following list of miniature and related publications may help you discover the world of miniatures.

A.I.M.M. Mott Miniature News
P.O. Box 5514
Sunny Hills Station
Fullerton, CA 92635
Annual; volume prices range from $9.00

Carstens Miniature Magazine
P.O. Drawer 700
Newton, NJ 07860
Annual: $1.00 per copy

Creating in Miniature
P.O. Box 2477
Little Rock, AR 72203
Bimonthly; $7.50 per year, $1.50 for sample copy

Creative Crafts
P.O. Drawer 700
Newton, NJ 07860
Bimonthly; $4.50 per year

Doll Castle News
P.O. Box 247
Washington, NJ 07882
Bimonthly; $5.50 per year, $1.00 for sample copy

Doll Reader
4701 Queensbury Road
Riverdale, MD 20840
Bimonthly; $4.95 per year

Dollhouse and Miniature News
3 Orchard Lane
Kirkwood, MO 63122
Monthly, except July and August; $8.50 per year, $1.00 for sample copy

Fantasy World
RD # 3
East Stroudsburg, PA 18301
Bimonthly; $5.00 per year

Milady in Miniature
12217 Fawnhaven Court
Woodmark
Ellicott City, MD 21043
Quarterly; $4.00 per year

Miniature Collector
Acquire Publishing Co.
170 Fifth Avenue
New York, NY 10010
Bimonthly; $12.00 per year

Miniature Magazine
P.O. Box 700
Newton, NJ 07860
Annual; $1.00 per issue

Miniature Makers Journal
409 South First Street
Evansville, WI 53536
Quarterly; $12.00 per year

National Association of Miniature Enthusiasts
Miniature Gazette
P.O. Box 2621
Brookhurst Center
Anaheim, CA 92804
Quarterly; $8.00 annual dues fee

Nutshell News
P.O. Box 1144
La Jolla, CA 92038
Quarterly; $7.00 per year

Paper Dolls and Paper Toys Quarterly Bulletin
c/o Barbara Jendrick
495 Mendon Road
Pittsford, NY 14534
Quarterly; $4.50 per year; $.50 for sample copy

The Scale Cabinet Maker
P.O. Box 87
Pembroke, VA 24136
Quarterly; $12.00 per year

Small Talk
c/o Jo Ann Jones
P.O. Box 334
Laguna, CA 92651
Monthly; $10.00 per year, $1.00 for sample
  copy

Society for Dollhouse Enthusiasts
State House Village
Scotch Plains, NJ 07076
Send self-addressed, stamped (two stamps)
  envelope for newsletter

Shaker Reading for Miniaturists

Andrews, Edward D. *Shaker Furniture*. New York: Dover Publications, 1950.

———. *Religion in Wood*. Bloomington: Indiana University Press, 1966.

———. *Community Industries of the Shakers*. Boston: Emporium Publications, 1972.

Handberg, Ejner. *Shop Drawings of Shaker Furniture and Woodenware*. Stockbridge: The Berkshire Traveller Press, 1973.

———. *Shop Drawings of Shaker Furniture and Woodenware, Volume II*. Stockbridge: The Berkshire Traveller Press, 1975.

———. *Shop Drawings of Shaker Iron and Tinware*. Stockbridge: The Berkshire Traveller Press, 1976.

Klamkin, Marian. *Hands to Work*. New York: Dodd, Mead and Company, 1972.

Meader, Robert F. W. *Illustrated Guide to Shaker Furniture*. New York: Dover Publications, 1972.

Melcher, Marguerite Fellows. *The Shaker Adventure*. Cleveland: The Press of Case Western Reserve University, 1968.

Mosher, Thomas. *How to Build Shaker Furniture*. New York: Drake Publishers, 1977.

Rose, Milton C. and Emily, editors. *A Shaker Reader*. New York: Universe Books (Main Street Press), 1977.

Shea, John G. *The American Shakers and Their Furniture*. New York: Van Nostrand Reinhold Company, 1971.

Sprigg, June. *By Shaker Hands*. New York: Alfred A. Knopf, 1975.

Index